TOUGH CALL

HARD-HITTING PHONE PRANKS

MIKE LOEW

ST. MARTIN'S GRIFFIN NEW YORK

TOUGH CALL. Copyright © 2000 by Mike Loew. All rights reserved. Printed in the United States of America, baby. No part of this book may be used or reproduced in any manner whatsoever without written permission except in the case of brief quotations embodied in critical articles or reviews. For information, address St. Martin's Press, 175 Fifth Avenue, New York, NY 10010.

Written, illustrated and designed by Mike Loew.

"The Meat Market," "Slave for a Day," "Holistic Healers," "Filling the Ranks," and "The Drug War" originally appeared in
The Onion and are copyright © 1995, 1995, 1996, 1996 and 1996 Onion, Inc.

Original design template by Scott K. Templeton.

Cover photo, photos on page 152, and original drawings on page 214 by Chad Nackers.

ISBN 0-312-26400-3

First St. Martin's Griffin Edition: May 2000

10 9 8 7 6 5 4 3 2 1

for the ladies

Chad Nackers and Scott Dikkers, for their contributions to this book; Scott Templeton, my guru of design; Anne and Scott Bogen, who designed my first book proposal; *The Onion* writers: Rob Siegel, John Krewson, Todd Hanson, Carol Kolb and Tim Harrod, who got nasty on speaker phone with me; Illa-Strait from the NSU crew; my original editors at *The Onion*, Stephen Thompson and Ben Karlin; my partner-in-rhyme with the fine drawing paper, Yohan Z. Blisster a.k.a. El Rapido; can't forget IK-47, Implodee-Z, Garth Vader, DJ Kitchen Sink, Astro-Celestial ET MCs and Curbscore Crew Worldwide; my *Onion* phone-prank forefathers, Graeme Zielinski and Kelly Ambrose; my parents, Jim and Mary Loew; my computer creator Andrew Welyczko; my personal trainer Dave Bogen; my incredible agent Daniel Greenberg; Elizabeth Beier, Scott Levine and Paul Wells at St. Martin's Press; my trio of high-powered attorneys: Ken Artis, esq., Paul Sleven, esq. and Joshua Rubins, esq.; and finally, all of the beautiful, innocent people who took time out of their busy day to talk with me. You are the true *Tough Call* heroes.

My advice to young reporters? Don't just be yourself. It's not enough. If you aspire to write truly unbiased news, you must trick and deceive your sources with an elaborate range of disguises. There's no better way to see all sides of a story. I discovered this cold-call secret early in my journalism career, when I began to mask myself as hundreds of different characters so I could ask the really tough questions—and get the really tough answers.

Some of these personas were easy to adopt, such as pretending to be a horny teenager in order to expose sexual incentives used by U.S. Navy recruiters. Other psyches that were more alien to my own demanded weeks of intense sensory deprivation to erase my personality, so that a new identity could be implanted by trained psycho-technicians. (Special thanks to Dr. Helmut Krieger, an expert living in Argentina who performed some of my trickiest ego transplants. Couldn't have done it without you, Helmut!)

But these calls were more than fun and games with old friends. Besides the wacky and humiliating multiple-personality mix-ups I often find myself in, I've angered a number of very powerful people with my work. I know that the Drug Enforcement Agency, the Serbian government, the Sony Robot Death Squad and one very prominent acupuncturist would all like to corner me in a dark alley. Mine is a pressure-cooker existence on the outer fringe of bad manners.

Some readers may not appreciate my aggressive reportage, finding these investigations to be "rude" or "illegal." Just remember—I wrote this book for our children. I had to interrupt the three basic scripts we all follow that shape 98 percent of human social interaction. I had to present people with unexpected experiences that they would never normally have. If I do not do these things, our social vocabulary, indeed, our very sense of human possibility will continue to shrink until we are all a twitching pair of eyeballs with a high-speed modem cable jacked into the base of our spines. Yes, I wrote this one for the kids.

The findings of these undercover investigations will shock you, but I think you can handle it. Just by picking up this book, you must be a reader that possesses a thirst for eternal truth, as well as your crucial $12.95. A quest for truth, with no consideration as to how it's obtained, is what you're holding right now. Every word in this book is from a real conversation, carefully transcribed to print. Their names have been changed, but the people I called could still be living right next door to you.

These dialogues are punctuated with the helpful Mikon™ Graphic System. Refer to these tiny drawings of my head if, at any point or for any reason, you forget the patterns of everyday human conversation. And now, one final piece of advice for those who wish to emulate me— move to the seething megalopolis that is Southern California. Nothing impresses people more than men who are able to say that they are truly calling from Los Angeles.

Veritas!

April 1, 2000

THE MEAT
MARKET

More Americans than ever are deciding to adopt a vegetarian diet, but this decision is by no means an easy one. While wrestling with his inner carnivore, Mike Loew turns to meat industry experts to justify his love for their delicious food products.

DER SAUSAGE HAUS

Hi, my name is Mike, and I'm calling you from Los Angeles because I'm in a tough situation. I think I need your help. Now, I love eating meat, but lately the vegetarian people have been getting to me. I've been hearing about the health risks of eating meat, and I'm wondering if you could help me stay true to beef.

Der Sausage Lady: Excuse me?

The vegetarian people have been talking about the dangers of eating meat, the contaminants in it, and I'm wondering if you could help me out, because I don't want my love affair with meat to end.

Uh-huh, right. So what would you like help with?

I want you to convince me to remain a meat-eater.

Me? Convince you? I think that's within yourself, sir. Our sausages are free of MSG and preservatives, that's all I can tell you.

Gosh, do they actually contain dead animals?

(sighs impatiently) Excuse me a minute.

Different Sausage Lady: Hello, can I help you?

Hi, my name is Mike, and I need help. A lot of vegetarian people have been talking to me about the dangers of eating meat, and I'm calling you to help me remain a meat-eater.

(emits amused chuckle) Well, that's personal preference, to become a meat-eater, but I don't see any proven studies that... I mean, your body needs meat, as well as it needs dairy, as well as it needs a few vegetables.

I've been worrying that I would be less manly if I don't eat meat. I mean, can you find many powerful hormones in a garden salad?

Well, I don't know about that. Maybe a chemist is the person you want to talk to, or a scientist or something. But I don't think that not eating meat makes you less of a man.

Well, that's good to know!

Not at all. (*chuckles*) Yes, meat's good for you, but you've got to eat up the whole food chain, and fish and everything. So people can't tell you that.

 That sounds delicious. Thank you!

Okay, bye-bye.

LARRY'S BUTCHER SHOP

 Hi, my name is Mike, and I'm calling you up from Los Angeles because I'm in a pretty sticky situation. Now I'm a meat-eater, but lately a lot of vegetarian people have been getting to me, talking about the dangers of eating meat. I'm calling some meat people, just trying to stay faithful to meat. I'm wondering if you can help me.

Larry: Well, what would you like to know?

 I'm wondering if it's true that many USDA meat inspectors don't let their children eat hamburgers anymore.

Totally untrue. In fact, meat consumption in general, especially beef, is up almost 3 percent this year.

 Wow.

Let me tell you a little bit. I don't know if you know the story about the situation that happened where the youngsters died by eating contaminated beef. I can tell you the story behind that.

 The story you won't read in the newspapers?

Well, the real story. Because those kinds of things that are printed bring concern to all of us. But let me tell you something: what was found inside of those hamburger patties was animal feces. Okay, that's something you didn't hear. That's where the sickness started from, and that's why the children died. They were eating waste materials. The meat inspector for the plant that sent these patties out thought it looked like almost a sabotage situation. Because the live animal comes in one end of the building, and the finished product is shipped from the opposite end of the building. And between these two ends of the building is a quality-control laboratory, which you have in all processing plants. For the waste products from the animal to get into the finished product on the opposite end of the building—and this is a building that employs roughly 3,000 employees—for that to happen, it almost had to be deliberate. And if that did happen, which is what they feel happened, somebody took as much as a ton of animal waste and dumped it into the finished product, which was ground and processed and frozen and shipped out. It should have been caught by the quality-control lab, but it was not.

Do you ever worry about eating animal feces?

Let me put it to you this way—there's restaurants that I supply that I would not eat at. But that has nothing to do with what they're buying. It has everything to do with how it's handled. If you're going to get sick from a restaurant, it's not going to be because the meat was bad. It's going to be because the meat was not handled properly. And it was tainted or it was old or something like that. I'm a fresh meat market. I don't sell anything frozen, because I never wanted anyone to say I'm hiding something because I'm freezing it.

Does that go on?

Certainly, it does. Large packing plants do that all the time. Where you're really going to get sick is the fast-food end of the restaurant business, because the majority of your burger joints are run by fifteen- and sixteen-year-old kids. Stop and think about that for a minute. They have absolutely no responsibility—and I have teenagers, so I know—and teenagers just don't take things as seriously as someone who's trying to make a career out of it. Now, I don't want to pick out any specific chains, but they're all in the same boat. They all have very young people running their businesses and they take what they can get. And they also buy the cheapest product out there. They're in business to make money, and a fast-food hamburger costs the restaurant only about three cents. So what do you expect to get for three cents? I don't expect to find a lot of quality in a quarter-pound of beef for three cents. You get what you pay for. If I needed my appendix out, and I got three different bids from three different doctors, I'm not so sure I would take the cheapest one. When I purchase product, I don't take the cheapest price. I buy quality and quality only. If the price has to be eight dollars a pound, then I'm sorry, it's gotta be eight dollars a pound. So that's a big thing to watch out for. Let me put it this way—I don't eat in restaurants because of the way food is handled. I haven't eaten fast food for fifteen years. And there are some very nice restaurants right here in town that I choose not to eat at, only because I've seen their kitchens and I've taken meat to many of these restaurants and had the privilege of going into their cooler to put the meat down. And I'm not stupid, I take a little look to see what's going on around me, and some of the things you see are pretty appalling. But it's not the meat! *(chuckles)*

You mean it's not the meat that's the problem, but what people do with their meat?

Exactly. That's the biggest concern. I grew up in the grocery and meat business my whole life, started out spreading sawdust on cooler floors in meat operations when I was eight years old, so I've seen a lot of changes. I'm forty-three years old, so I've seen a lot of changes in the business. But let me tell you, the problem isn't the meat. If you had a cancer-infected black Angus steer, that piece of meat is going to eat real tough and it's going to have a bitter taste. But even if you ate the tumor itself, it's not going to make you sick.

No?

No! It's going to pass through your system like anything else, and you're going to get up from the table and say, "Geez, that was a lousy-tasting piece of meat, and it was really tough and chewy." But on the other hand, if that piece of meat is spoiled, it's rancid, and you eat it, then you're going to get sick. So those are the things I'm concerned about, and those are the things I think you as a consumer should be very concerned about. If you go into a meat market and there's an odor, or if you approach certain meat operations in grocery stores and you can smell a distinct odor, if that odor isn't bleach I wouldn't buy anything there. Because bleach is something that is used an awful lot in good meat operations to clean all the equipment that the meat is processed on, and that is far more important than anything else. If you never smell a little hint of bleach, and you smell other odors, that meat department is not clean. That would concern me. But the product coming in the back door of that department is perfectly fine.

So you've been in slaughterhouses?

Oh, gosh, yes.

Are they all that bad?

Slaughterhouses are not the neatest places in the whole world to spend a lot of time, but you've got to remember that they have a real lousy job to do. I mean, killing and processing animals is not really that much fun.

 Do they actually kill the animals there?

Oh, the animals are killed at the slaughterhouse, yes. But like I said, with normal procedures, and the rinsing and the washing of the carcasses after they're processed, those are all things that make it very, very... It's pretty hard to contaminate a piece of meat.

 Really?

I'll be honest with you. It's not like doing brain surgery, okay? You have to really go out of your way to cause a piece of meat to spoil.

 I've heard stories about certain organs being taken out of animals and intestinal waste spilling onto the meat—

It's not so much the intestinal waste as it is the urine bag. If you break the urine bag during slaughter, and it drips down on the meat, the meat that it dripped on should be disposed of. It's not something you can wash off and fix, because the urine penetrates the muscle tissue and stays right in the meat. But again, if you ate that, you're not going to get sick. I don't care what kind of a digestive sensitivity you have, you're not going to get sick. But you're not going to be happy, either. You're not going to say, "I just had the best steak I ever had." You're going to say, "That steak tasted like liver." You know if you've had liver that it has a very distinct smell and a very distinct taste. Now if you ever eat a piece of beef, the piece of beef that would be most susceptible to this would be the beef tenderloin. Because the beef tenderloin rests right next to the liver. And it also rests right next to the urine bag itself. And if that bag is broken during the slaughter process, the tenderloin, because the animal is hanging upside down, the tenderloin is going to be the piece of meat that gets totally saturated with urine. When that happens, it's going to taste like liver. So if you've ever been in a restaurant and ordered a beef tenderloin that has a slight hint of a liver taste or smell, it's been tainted. And again, it won't make you sick, but it's going to be more like eating a piece of liver than a tenderloin. But I think your concerns are wonderful. If I were you I would never stop eating meat because everything in moderation will be tolerable. If you're worried about getting sick from e. coli or salmonella, what you have to do is just take some normal precautions. Ninety-nine-point-nine percent of it is common sense. Now if you want to be concerned about something, be concerned about the poultry industry. There's a lot less regulation in the poultry industry than the beef industry.

Countries from all over the world come to us for our cattle. For instance, I don't even allow ketchup in my house. Because I want my kids to appreciate the true taste of beef. If they want to have french fries with ketchup that's fine, but not on good beef.

 You sound like a true meat lover, sir.

That's right. No ketchup on my meat. Learn to appreciate it the way it's supposed to be.

 It does have that flavor that I love and I would love to remain true to it.

You know what you gotta do is be concerned with how stuff is handled. Take a look at where you eat, that would be the best advice I could give you. I could go on for about a day, telling you about different situations and different things, but all in all, believe me, the meat in this country, it's not the fault of the meat. And if you ever want a first-class ground sirloin that you can take home and make burgers out of, you come on down and see me, and I'll be more than glad to give you the best that you can buy.

THE BEEF COUNCIL

 Hi, this is Mike, and I'm calling from Los Angeles. I'm in a tough situation here. Now, I eat meat—I love hamburgers, I love ribs, I love pork knuckles—but I've been wondering about all the stuff the vegetarian people have been telling me lately. They've been talking about the health risks, and I'm wondering if you can help me out in remaining a meat-eater. I called a butcher just now because I'm really troubled by this problem.

Female Beef Councillor: Who did you call?

 I talked to Larry at Larry's Butcher Shop. He was an awfully nice guy, and he recommended that I call you.

Well, there's a couple of things. Just addressing your concerns, what have you been hearing? Are you interested in nutrition?

 Well, I'm concerned about the health risks. I've read how federal regulations are relaxed now so that more cows are going through the slaughtering process quicker than ever. Then gross stuff gets in the meat, which makes children die after eating hamburgers at a

Jack In The Box restaurant.

Yes, but to address some of your questions on health and nutrition in eating beef, I can show you a lot of documentation from dieticians, from the USDA, showing that beef has about six grams of fat in a three-ounce cooked portion, and that easily fits into the American Heart Association guidelines for eating meat. I don't know you, but I can give you a ballpark figure—you should eat about forty grams of fat a day, and think of that when you're adding up your fat grams. But blanket regulations on nutrition don't apply to everyone. For example, I have very low cholesterol, so I don't need to worry about cholesterol.

 I'm in the same boat, actually. I'm pretty thin, so I don't have to worry about cholesterol? That really eases the mind.

Everything in moderation. Even a cream puff at the state fair, I always say, if you have one a year, you're fine. Eating a variety of fruits and vegetables, meat and dairy products, grains, everything in the pyramid.

 But do you think it would be a bad idea to stop eating meat?

It all depends on your personal choice. I don't have any problem with that. I don't want people telling me what to eat. I can just give you the facts, and you have to make that decision.

 Right. It's up to me, I guess. (sighs) I've been thinking about reading The Jungle, by Upton Sinclair. Do you think that would be a good idea?

I haven't read that book. I've heard about it, but I have not read it. I have a lot of other books I've read recently I could recommend to you. I just read The Celestine Prophecy, and I just read all of John Grisham's books.

 Is there much about meat in those?

No. I mean, there's meat in the content of the books, they're good books, but no beef, pork, lamb or veal. (laughs)

 O-kay. Well, this issue can tug at the heartstrings, you know? Once I was driving in Wyoming real late at night on a road trip, and I stopped for some gas, and there was a trailer full of cows next to me. And they were transporting them to the slaughterhouse at night

so no one could hear them all screaming. Do you think those screaming cows somehow had an innate foreknowledge of their own death?

I have never heard a cow scream, and I worked on a farm for years. They are a food product, and Americans love the taste of them, so as long as Americans love the taste of beef, producers will continue to produce it.

How do you feel about tofu?

I like tofu. I have a recipe for tofu cheesecake that's really good.

Do you ever wonder about the costs of beef? The American public demands it, but isn't the rain forest being cut down to make grazing land for McDonald's?

No, actually, McDonald's buys all their beef in the United States.

Are the other big chains like that?

Not all of them. I think Wendy's has a sign up that says they buy all their beef in the U.S., but as far as the rain forest goes, people love to blame that on beef, but it's really a human and political issue. It's humans that are cutting down the rain forest, not the cattle. And a lot of times, what's happening is that they're clearing that beautiful, wonderful rain forest unfortunately and producing crops that are very poor-yielding. That land is not meant for producing crops or grazing cattle. I or you alone are unable to stop what other countries are doing, and the fact that they do not consider beautiful rain forest valuable is an issue that's bigger than you or I.

Do you think one way to oppose that on an individual level would be to stop eating meat?

No, because it wouldn't have any effect. The United States currently exports meat. We have plenty of meat to feed our country. The argument that the rain forests are being cleared for beef is absurd, because we don't import any meat from South America, because of a disease that they have down there. And it's illegal for beef to come into our country from their country, so our cattle don't get it. Most of the beef that is imported into the United States comes from other countries, like Australia. So the rain forest issue doesn't have any effect. And they're growing soybeans on that land, so should people stop eating tofu? It's not going to make any difference. They're raising those products for their own people, and unfortunately the political climate is such that the people themselves can't get them to stop.

 Hmm.

I love tree frogs as much as you do. The beef industry is made out to be the big bad guy on that issue, and we are not. It doesn't make any sense.

 So calling cows "hoofed locusts" is out of line?

Yes, it is.

 Okay. It sounds like you really know what you're talking about.

Thank you. And if you have any more questions, feel free to give me a call.

Mike Loew now subsists exclusively on a diet of grade-A American beef.

AERIAL ADVERTISING FIRM

 Hi, my name is Mike Loew and I'm calling from Los Angeles. So, you guys do the banners that trail from the backs of planes?

Male Aerial Advertiser: Yup, yup.

 I have a special message that I wanted to have flying over our company picnic next month. I was wondering if we could put the words "Fuck You, Brent" on a sign and fly it up there.

What was that?

 Well, pardon my language, but the words would be "Fuck You, Brent." It's for this guy named Brent that I really hate.

I couldn't put that on there.

 Aw, c'mon.

Nope, I'm sorry.

 You can't do it? Is there a law against it?

Yup, yup, profanity you can't do.

 Really? I could tone it down a little bit. Could we do a "Kiss My Ass, Brent"?

I couldn't do that, either! No, when you get these licenses, profanity is not allowed. Otherwise, I'd lose the license.

 Geez. Isn't that public air space? What's the big deal?

I know, but you're still advertising like that, and you can't do it.

 Do you know of any other aerial advertisers that are more edgy?

I don't know... Maybe you can try the guy down in Rockford. Call the airport down there and find out who that guy is.

 He's more of a rude, Chicago kind of guy?

Yeah, Rockford, Illinois. I know there's a guy down there.

Okay. Do you do any other kind of aerial advertising? Maybe we could send up an unmanned balloon with the "Fuck You, Brent" on it, and then they couldn't track you down, since you're not actually flying it.

No, no, all I do is pull the banners. Okay?

 Oh well. It would have been great. Thanks anyway.

SLAVE

FOR A DAY

Temporary job placement agencies exist to provide employment to suit the short-term needs of both employers looking for fast labor and employees looking for quick income. While the pay is generally adequate, the work is usually less than cerebral. Mike Loew, in an investigative effort to expose any slave-trading in the temporary employment industry, placed clandestine phone calls to top agencies and attempted to buy healthy workers to do his bidding.

READYTEMPS

 Hi, this is Mike and I'm calling from Los Angeles. I'm looking for about five or ten healthy males.

Dave at ReadyTemps: Five to ten. Okay.

 Race is not important to me. Want to make that clear.

Right.

 That's an eighteenth-century notion.

Of course. How soon before you need these people?

 Next few days.

And what kind of work will they be doing?

 General labor. Whatever should happen to come up. You know, I just want people there to do what I tell them.

All-righty. I'm going to have Ron call you back on this one. Now you don't need all these at one time, I take it?

 No.

Up to five or ten people you're looking to hire?

 That's right.

What's the heaviest stuff they're going to be lifting, roughly? Like haying and stuff like that?

 Boy, as far as the heaviest, I don't know. Whatever they're capable of, I can find stuff for them to lift.

Right.

 Now, you're saying you don't deal in this area? You need to talk to somebody else?

Well, yeah, that's my boss. We need to talk about this, come up with the rate on this. How many would you be needing at a time? As far as working?

I was hoping to get my hands on the five or ten, like I said.

But like five now and five later, or—

 I was hoping to buy them all at once.

Okay. But you want to meet these people first.

 I definitely want to take a look at them, yes.

Okay. Ron will be getting back to you by this afternoon.

TEMP BEST SERVICES

 Mike from Los Angeles here. I need some laborers.

Sue at Temp Best Services: What will they be doing?

 All-purpose help. Farming.

Will there be any tools, or...

 There will be nothing skilled. Nothing I can't train them to do.

Okay, just for our knowledge and to explain the job to them, what are they harvesting?

 I'm a standard crop-rotation property, so it changes every year. This year it's alfalfa.

So will they be using some kind of a knife?

 Yeah. Or bare hands. *(pause on other end of line)* **Now, how much do they cost, exactly?**

Well, I'm going to have to run this by my manager to see what he's thinking. I need some more information first. How many people do you think you're going to need?

 Five males and maybe ten or fifteen females, for breeding.

For what?

For breeding.

And what is that?

 You know, if I want more, later on. *(long pause)* Hello?

You're breeding?

 Yes.

As in, like, mating?

 That's right.

We're a staffing agency, with people.

 Right.

I don't think we can help you.

 Do you know of any other agencies who might...

(Sue hangs up)

ABLE TEMPS

 Hi, this is Mike calling from Los Angeles. I'm looking for some slaves for my business. Do you think you could help me out?

Joyce at Able Temps: Okay, I do the secretarial permanent placement. We would be able to get laborers for you. They'd probably go with you on a temp-to-hire basis then. Helen, in our temporary department, is on the phone with another client right now, but if you hold on—

 Okay, but I'm wondering, what are the state laws regarding treatment of these types of employees?

They'd be our employees if they're temping for us. I'm not sure of the legalities on how much they can lift or anything like that.

 I was thinking more in terms of punishment.

I'm not sure what you mean.

Well, let's say one of them ran away and I had to punish him. What would the state laws be regarding how far I could go?

Oh, just firing them?

 Firing them is all I could do?

You might be better off explaining this to somebody in temporary with regard to laborers. Helen's off the phone now. One moment.

Helen: Hello, this is Helen.

 I want to buy about five or ten people. Healthy males. How much would that cost me?

Well, I'm in temporary services, and what we do is first we would bill you and take care of taxes and unemployment, worker's comp, and a service fee for providing these people.

 So is there a way I could just pay you outright and not have to deal with that stuff?

Well, then that would be a permanent placement. Let's say you wanted a worker. We'd scan candidates, maybe fax resumes or arrange interviews, or however you wanted to do it.

 Like an auction.

Pardon?

 Well, I'd have several to choose from, right?

Right. And when you decided on a candidate, then there would be a one-time fee.

 So after I pay the fee, who owns them, you or me?

You. If you pay the fee, then they're yours and we have nothing more to do with them.

 That's awesome.

Let me send you to someone in that department who can help you.

Anne: This is Anne. How may I help you?

Hi, I need five or ten strong males on a permanent basis.

Okay, can you tell me what you were looking at paying those people?

 Well, I was hoping for about five or ten thousand apiece.

Five or ten thousand?

 Right.

Per year?

 No, total.

Are you saying an annual salary?

 No, I mean I give you five or ten thousand dollars, and those people are mine.

(*pause*) How many hours are you talking about?

 Well, no specific hours. I was thinking they'd be on call. You know, live right on the property.

Well, let me explain to you how we do this. If you want people to come out on a permanent basis, we can do it one of two ways. We can find you people and send them out to you. They will work for about three months. We will charge you a bill rate, and then we will pay their salary. We will pay employer's taxes, worker's comp and unemployment tax. And then after three months if you decide you want those people, then they would be yours at no fee.

 That sounds like a good arrangement.

As far as taking a person on a permanent placement, what we would do is charge you a percent of their annual salary. If you're looking at this many people, we can probably do something more for you. The only problem—

 So you're talking about some kind of bargain rate?

Yes. And we're extremely flexible with that.

 Sounds great.

The only problem I'm seeing is that there could be a worker's compensation issue here. Because we do have certain rules regarding what our people can and cannot do.

 Like what?

We don't allow them to go over eight feet high. We don't allow them to go so many feet down, and I can't remember exactly what that is.

 So you're saying no digging, and no roofing?

Right. Things that go over eight feet.

 Well, that limits me. I was hoping to have all-purpose people that I could have do pretty much anything I told them.

Well, if you come in and hire those people right away as an immediate placement, then that is not an issue.

 Excellent.

On the other hand, if you go to a temporary person and try them out for hire, then we cannot have those people out doing things that are not safe, what we call meeting our safety qualifications.

 So those people, those temporary people, they're not slaves?

That's right. And on top of that, it's important to us that our people are always safe. If somebody gets hurt on our payroll, we're liable for worker's compensation.

 Then I think I'll go for those permanent ones you described before. I think they're everything a master could want.

Okay, let me get your name and address, and we'll see what we can do for you.

Mike Loew is now the proud owner of five strapping men.

INTERNET SERVICE PROVIDER

 Hello, I am a poor young boy from Algeria and I need a Web site.

Internet Service Man: Okay, when you say Web site, you mean a personal Web site, or one that would have a domain name?

 Yes, my village needs an e-commerce site.

I can talk to you about this, but you'll have to put an application through for secure server access. Are you looking at any particular plan that we're offering for the businesses?

 I am not sure what plans you have. My hope and dream is to have a site where I can sell my handicrafts.

Okay, and you're doing this with a credit card?

 I do not have such a thing. But I dream of sharing in people's credit cards from around the world.

Well, essentially, let me tell you two different programs that we have here. We have a plan called the Prestige Plan, that gives you unlimited access on one e-mail account, for $34.95 a month. Also, it gives you ten megabytes of storage space for your Web site. We do have another plan, called the Business Plan, that gives you also unlimited access on one e-mail account, for $49.95, but it gives twenty-five megabytes of storage space for the Web site, and if you sign up on the Business Plan, there is no set-up, there is no fee for the secure server access. But if you do do it through the Prestige Plan, there's a $75 set-up fee for that particular plan, it's what they call a secure certificate.

 Yes, and do I need to have my own computer first, and then you make my site?

Yeah, what you would do is... do you have a Web designer, or are you going to be designing the site?

 I was hoping to make it myself, with my family's time-honored tradition of fine handiwork. We make beautiful hand-carved trinkets from the bones of a goat.

Okay, so essentially you would have to create the entire site, and then once we have everything set up on our server, you'd be able to transfer all the files onto our server, onto the server space that we would have allocated for you. And the other thing is that you would have to have a domain name registered, there's a couple of fees involved with that as well.

 Oh, no.

For registering a domain name, it's $70 for the first two years of ownership of the domain name, that's through a company called InterNIC, kind of like the worldwide registry of domain names.

 Seventy dollars?

Correct. And then there's another fee for us, essentially the domain name registration and putting the domain name on our server, which is $100, that's a one-time fee as well.

 Oh, there are so many fees.

Correct. Correct. For example, if you're doing Prestige Plan, there's the $100 fee, for setting up the domain name on our server, there's the $75 fee from InterNIC, for registering the domain name and the ownership of it for two years, then there'd be the $75 fee for your secure server certificate, which would be essentially what you need for you to do transactions online with that. And then there's also a one-time fee of $25 for creating the Prestige Plan in itself, it's a dial-up set-up fee, so, you're looking like, on a Prestige Plan, you'd be looking at $270 a month in upstart costs, and then it would $34.95 a month.

 And how much is a computer machine?

That really varies depending on where exactly you buy it from and whatnot. So we do have a company called Computers 'n' Stuff, and I can give you that phone number.

 Do they give extra computers away to poor boys?

They sell. They sell computers there. And the number there is (*provides number*).

 Thank you, sir. Can you help me make my Web site, please?

Uh, I can't, but there's quite a few different companies out there that can help you with it. So, do you have access to e-mail currently?

No, I do not. My village does not have many telephones.

Because I do know of a Web designer, but he's accessible by e-mail only.

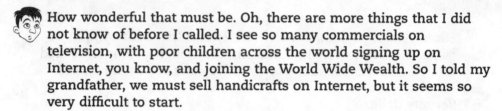 How wonderful that must be. Oh, there are more things that I did not know of before I called. I see so many commercials on television, with poor children across the world signing up on Internet, you know, and joining the World Wide Wealth. So I told my grandfather, we must sell handicrafts on Internet, but it seems so very difficult to start.

Yeah, you would essentially have to have a connection to make it.

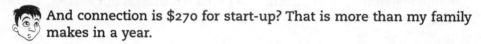 And connection is $270 for start-up? That is more than my family makes in a year.

Yeah, that's the upstart costs, you would have a monthly fee of $34.95 after that.

 Yes, so I need to make site first, then I talk to you?

Yeah, you'd also want to get the computer and get yourself acquainted with the Internet as well, that's another thing you'd have to take into consideration.

 Yes, but I am not sure where to find computers here—

I can give you the phone number for our sister company, that sells computers, it's *(provides number again)*.

 Yes, that is the same number.

All right? *(rising in pitch)*

 Would you like to buy a handicraft so I can save for my computer?

No, thank you. Okay? *(vocal pitch ratchets up another notch)*

 I understand. Thank you for welcoming me into the Information Age.

Happy to help! 'Bye.

HOLISTIC
HEALERS

Today's health-care consumer is faced with a baffling number of alternatives to traditional medical treatment. In an effort to inform and enlighten, Mike Loew presents an array of medical questions to a variety of holistic practitioners. Their ancient healing wisdom holds many answers for us all.

HEALER #1: YOGA CENTER

 Hi, I'm calling from Los Angeles with a problem I think yoga could help me with. I was roller-blading today, and a bus cut me off. I took a pretty bad spill, and now I have this bone sticking out of my arm. I was wondering if there are any yoga exercises that could slowly, gently work that bone back into my body.

Male Yoga Instructor: Give me the, uh, tell me more about it.

 I wiped out and fell right on my arm, and it's near the elbow, this bone that's sticking out. It's... unsightly.

Not sticking out through the skin, is it?

 Yeah. *(emits grunt of pain)*

So this bone is sticking out through the skin. Have you seen a doctor?

 No, it just happened today.

Okay, what do you need?

 Some sort of yoga technique that could gently work that bone back into my body.

Which bone is it, near the elbow? The humerus?

 It's one of the long bones in my forearm.

Your forearm. The radius, or the ulna?

 One of those two. Maybe both. There's just a lot of bone jutting out below my elbow. Blood too. Lots of it.

Do you have any insurance?

 No. I'm more into herbs and stuff.

I would still recommend you see a doctor for that. Anything that's penetrating outside the protective skin layer is something I would recommend you see a doctor for.

 So there's no simple breathing exercises I could do?

Oh, yeah, you can do a lot with that, but I'd have to see you, and I don't have the time today. And I'm gone until Monday. I'm going on a mini-vacation after the Mother Earth festival, so I won't be able to see you this week at all. But I would recommend you call Perfect Lotus Yoga Center, and ask Steve about it. He would know something about it. But he'll tell you the same thing—go see a doctor.

So you don't have any big secrets of yoga for me.

Are you a yoga student already?

I'm an amateur enthusiast. I haven't taken any classes, but I've done some reading on my own.

Well, at your level of expertise, I wouldn't recommend it, I'd recommend seeing a doctor.

Would more powerful yogis be able to deal with something like this?

I'm not available, but if I was, I would see you right now. But someone could help you shorten the healing time on that.

Thanks, man.

HEALER #2: REIKI CLINIC

Hi, this is Mike from Los Angeles and I'm interested in reiki massage. It's a study of energy, and how to move energy through the body, right?

Female Reiki Practitioner: Yes.

I'm wondering if I could use those techniques to take energy out of other people for myself.

It isn't an energy that you take from me or I give to you, it's a channeled energy.

Within my own system?

It's a universal energy. Once you've been trained in reiki, you can do it on yourself, yes.

Basically, I have the need for large amounts of energy.

Uh-huh.

 And I'm wondering if I could tap into the energy field of a human or other animal, and drain their energy away to increase my own power.

Well, that's not exactly how it works. But you could tap into an energy form, and it's very powerful and beneficial. Have you ever experienced reiki?

 No, I've just read about it. But it sounds like something I could use for my plans.

I can do it for you. I do it in the salon here, and I could give you a session. I'm working on my reiki master, but I do know one who teaches, then it's something you can do for yourself. It isn't so much tapping off of other people—that would be like being an energy vampire.

 Exactly.

The problem with that is you don't know what you're picking up when you take someone else's energy. This is really a purer, higher form of energy than what you would get secondhand from someone else. When I do it, I tap into this energy source, and it flows through me, and the longer you do it, the more you can feel blockages in people. And if you have a great need for it, some people just pull more energy. But I would say try the reiki, try a treatment or two, and see how you feel with that, and I can connect you with my reiki master. And I would say this to you, too—this is my experience—first degree reiki is good, it's like a glow, but the second degree is more of a laser.

 So could I focus that laser to destroy my enemies?

No. This is only an energy that you use for good purposes. It doesn't work for a negative.

 Are there any other holistic practices that would enable me to drain energy from other humans and use it to destroy things?

No.

Any kind of dark yoga, or—

That's not what I'm involved in, so I really couldn't tell you. But you realize you get that back tenfold if you throw that out there.

Laws of karma?

Oh yeah, lots of karma and lots of negative energy. You almost sound like you want to practice an occult art, but even in an occult art, I don't know anybody that would teach you something negative. Simply because of the repercussions of it, which are pretty negative on you.

That doesn't bother me.

I don't know what you want to do, but basically reiki is used for healing. I don't know of any negative application of it, period. It doesn't work that way. I would think twice before sending something like that out. Eventually the repercussions will come back to you and unless you're really a master at it, there is a price to be paid for that. Karmically and psychically, the implications of taking someone's energy are pretty negative.

You don't think that would make me stronger?

Make you stronger? It would also make you pretty evil.

I've always been sort of evil. It's just the way I am.

Then I don't know if I can help you, since I'm really not into that stuff.

That's too bad. Do you know of any other reiki practitioners who are more evil, ma'am?

No.

Fine. Thank you for your time. Have a lovely day.

HEALER #3: FLOWER ESSENCES

Hi, I'm calling from Los Angeles because I was cleaning my gun, and it went off, and I shot myself in the foot. Can I get some help from your clinic?

Female Doctor of Flower Essences: Uh, you should call a regular clinic.

 I'm sort of against traditional medicine. I'm wondering if there's any sort of natural way to—

Well, have you pierced your foot with a bullet?

 Yeah, it's bleeding and stuff.

Right, I think you should go to a conventional clinic. You've got a hole in your foot. That requires basic, allopathic care.

 After that, do you think there's any sort of delicate flower essence that could help me?

Well, there might be some kind of homeopathic remedy, depending on what's been damaged. Broken bones, muscle, whichever part of the foot's been damaged. Can you tell at this point?

 There's just a big hole on the top there. Whoo, that smarts. Is there any sort of gentle stretching I could do before I get to the doctor?

No, there's nothing I would recommend. If you have a homeopathic remedy arnica, you could take that.

 A what?

Arnica, a homeopathic arnica.

 What is that?

It's a homeopathic medicine. If you don't have that, you should just go to the emergency room.

 If I had that homeopathic medicine, would that help me?

It might help with the pain, from an injury like that, but you need to have that wound bandaged, whatever else.

 I was thinking about directing some chi energy down to the foot, to heal it quicker. Any tips on that?

For one thing, I don't give tips over the phone. You've pierced your body with a bullet, so you either go see somebody for it, or if you're really intent on not doing that... Have you pierced your body before with a bullet?

Came damn close a few times, but yeah, this is my first.

Okay, I've never treated anything like that, so I'm not going to say, "Just do this and it'll be fine." You could get an infection, and it could be serious, so either you'd have to come in and see me, for alternative... Okay, here's what I can tell you. Go to the conventional clinic, see what they say. I can give you alternatives to something like antibiotics, if they insist on that. If they would want to give you pain medicine—I don't know how much pain you're in—I could give you alternatives to that. Perhaps I could give you a remedy or two that would help with the healing process. But I think you should have it looked at. That sounds like a major trauma. You might need a bone set, or minor surgery to close the wound. I don't do minor surgery at my practice. Once you get that done, if you want alternatives for prevention of infection for the wound, or pain medication, I'd be glad to help you out with that.

Okay, let me wipe some of this up here. I was hoping the flowers could help me, but I guess I could go to the doctor and check it out.

Right. Give me a call if you want any advice after that.

Appreciate that.

Okay, bye-bye.

HEALER #4: NATURE'S PANTRY

Hi, my name is Mike, and I'm calling because all of my friends say that I'm really stupid, and I was hoping to find some pills or herbs that could make me smarter.

Female Store Owner: Okay, the first thing you want to get is a book called *Brain Longevity.*

And that would make my brain longer?

No, it will make you smarter. It will educate you about the brain. And, of course, it's a whole lifestyle change that he recommends, including yoga, changing your diet, and certain supplements. The brain is flesh and blood, and needs to be maintained and fed properly. You need essential fatty acids, you need things like lecithin, there's a couple of things called phosphatidyl-serine, phosphatidyl-choline—

Whoa, you've got to spell those out for me, ma'am.

Let me go get the book, and then I can give you the name of the author.

(on hold)

Hi, the book is called *Brain Longevity*, and it's by Dharma Singh Khalsa, M.D.

Ha ha, his name sounds funny.

Actually, he's really great. I'm about halfway through the book, and I'm really impressed.

Oh, are you getting smarter?

I hope so. I'm also dealing with migraines, which create a brain-fog, which is really frustrating. Okay, the phosphatidyl-choline is spelled P-H-O-S-P-H-A-T-I-D-Y-L-C-H-O-L-I-N-E.

Could I buy that phospho stuff at your store?

Oh, definitely.

What else can I do? You mentioned yoga—are there some cool moves that would make me smarter?

Definitely. What you're after is brain nourishment, and brain circulation, and certain breathing techniques and yoga can bring circulation to the brain. You can also bring back cognitive function—if you've lost some, it can be brought back.

The thing is, I've always been really stupid, since I was a dumb little baby. Can I rise up a few smartness levels with this book?

Definitely, definitely. He also has mental as well as physical exercises, it's a whole program, it's really great. It's recommended by Dr. Andrew Weil, I don't know if you know him, but he's a very well-known natural doctor, so an endorsement by him is great.

En-dorse-ment?

Yes, Andrew Weil is a very respected doctor, and when he says it's a good book, that's an endorsement. Okay, I have to go now.

 Okay, I can wait.

No, I have to wait on a customer here.

 Sure, I'll just hold. *(Nature's Pantry hangs up)* Hello?

HEALER #5: ACUPUNCTURE CLINIC

 Hi, I'm calling from out of town on my dairy farm here. I've got forty head of cattle, and one of the cows is in some trouble. She's been shaking, convulsing, lotta mucus running out of the eyes. Something wrong there for sure, so I'm wondering if I can put some acupuncture to work on that animal.

Male Acupuncturist: I am not qualified to work on cows. I just work on people. There are some veterinary acupuncturists... Where is your farm?

 I'm out by Wausaukeewego here.

I'm not sure where that is.

 It's about three hours north of Shiocton.

I see.

 So could you send me a chart here, with some cattle energy meridians, so I could try my hand at this?

No, I couldn't. I don't have a chart like that, and it probably wouldn't be appropriate for you to amateurishly try to apply acupuncture.

 Hey, I'm not trying to cut in on your business here, pal. But I can feel the energy running through those cows. I spend a lot of time with them, because I'm unmarried, ya know.

Okay.

And I did try sticking a few pins in one of the cattle, and I did get a response. But you don't think it's a good idea to plunge forward and see what happens?

Uh, no. I would recommend a veterinary acupuncturist.

 I did see an acupuncture special on "20/20."

I'm sorry, that's all I can do for you. I have a patient and I have to get back. I hope your cow gets better.

 Okay, you have a good one, buddy.

HEALER #6: LIFESTREAM CLINIC

 Hi, this is Mike and I'm calling from Los Angeles. My girlfriend Mandy left me, and I'm wondering if there's any natural treatments for a broken heart.

Female Healer: Well, if you want to come in, we do a lot of work with depression and those kinds of things.

 That's me. What sort of procedures do you do?

We offer quite a number of options. Acupuncture is a possibility, with or without needles. Flower essences are very good, herbs are a possibility, aromatherapy is a possibility. So there's quite a number of options.

 Okay. What kind of aroma would be good for my problem? Just don't say lavender, because Mandy used a shampoo with that in it.

I wouldn't prescribe anything without seeing you.

 In other cases like this, has there been any kind of aroma or herb that seems to help?

It depends on the person, and your situation. There is no one thing that's good for everybody.

 Except love.

Mm-hmm. Would you want to book an appointment at this time?

I'm just calling around right now for options. I'm just sitting on the couch here, eating some chips.

We have very good success rates with depression. We work with a lot of people who have been put on antidepressants, and we've had great success with those people.

 How would flower essences help? Are they powerful, concentrated—

Actually not powerful—they're very diluted, but they have the right vibration that would neutralize other vibrations that are throwing you off kilter. That's how they work, through electromagnetic vibrations.

 That reminds me, when Mandy and I were listening to the Beach Boys once, we—

Yeah, we might use gem tincture, I might give you breathing exercises, I might give you dietary therapy, we offer quite a number of options here. Then we can pick and choose what's right for you. No two people are alike, and that's why I'm hesitant to make any suggestions. We need to see what your pattern is.

With his newly acquired knowledge of the energy field that flows through all humans, Mike Loew sent a wave of orgasmic energy up his spinal column to explode in his brain.

SONY

 Listen, I bought your robot dog AIBO and it's gone completely berserk! It chased the children up the tree in the backyard, and now it's running around outside screeching and howling!

Sony Female: Oh my god, I'm so sorry! Please hold.

(on hold)

Different Sony Female: Sony Electronics, may I help you?

 You've got to help me! I bought the Sony robot dog, but it chased my children up the tree, and now it's growling at my back door! What do I do?!?

Okay, call *(provides a 1-800 number)*.

 You can't help me at all? Its red glowing eyes are so frightening!

Sir, I don't know anything about the dog.

 OH CHRIST, IT'S IN THE HOUSE!!!

Thank you for calling, sir.

SONY 1-800 LINE

Recorded voice: Thank you for calling the Sony AIBO Adoption Line. Please stay on the line, and the next available representative will be with you shortly.

(uplifting soft jazz)

Thank you for holding. Please remain on the line, and the next available representative will be with you shortly.

(uplifting soft jazz)

Thank you for holding. Please remain on the line, and the next available representative will be with you shortly.

(uplifting soft jazz and metallic chewing sounds)

OUR WEIGHT PROBLEM

We can all take pride in the fact that America is the best-fed nation on the planet. However, our world superiority in per-capita caloric consumption does not come without a price. Food surplus afflictions can range from mild, such as indigestion, to serious, such as death for people who are really huge. In order to empathize with those who are unable to leave their bedrooms, Mike Loew packed 800 pounds onto his previously thin frame to learn first-hand what these Americans must endure.

MULTINATIONAL SNACK CORPORATION

(The names of snack products have been changed to protect Mike Loew.)

Hi, my name is Mike. I love the awesome crunch of your Zestito™ chips, but I weigh over 900 pounds, and I can't leave my bedroom. I was hoping that you could deliver chips to my home every day like you do to grocery stores in the area.

Male Snack Provider: I'm sorry, but we have had problems with that in the past.

What kind of problems?

I've only been with the company a little while, but I know that some route salespersons have had problems with being accosted when delivering to homes.

I couldn't accost anyone. I can't leave my reinforced waterbed.

I know that you couldn't, but we have had those problems. And I'm certainly not pointing the finger at you—don't misunderstand me.

All right. Were your drivers attacked by people desperate to get their hands on your tasty chips?

There was a variety of incidents. But for your question, I would suggest maybe a neighbor, a friend, a relative...

Yeah, my mother has been bringing me my chips, but she's getting older, and I thought that I should take some responsibility for myself.

We unfortunately cannot do that for you. I wish we could, but we cannot.

Please? I only need about forty bags a day, especially the Cool Tang™ flavor. It's becoming difficult for my mother to get all those chips to me, and I was hoping that a truck could just pull up and drop them off. How about dropping them off at the front door? We could set up a payment plan—

No, no, there's a prohibition for the route salespersons on that.

I would never hurt anyone who brought me Zestitos™.

I understand. Maybe you could get Meals On Wheels to do something for you. Maybe they would pick up a case for you.

 That's a possibility. I'm one of those guys, you know, to get me out of here, you'd have to cut the wall away. I don't know what to do...

Well, we cannot do it. I wish I could help you, but I cannot. All right, sir?

 I'm just trying to think of another way to get those chips. They're a big part of my life. To state the obvious, you guys are doing great work here.

All right, sir, thank you so much.

 No, thank you.

FORKLIFT COMPANY

 Hi, I'm at 924 North Washington Street, and I need a ride to the Cub Foods on the east side.

Forklift Man: This is a forklift company.

 Well, I'm a very heavy man, I'm just over 900 pounds—

Really?

 Okay, okay, I'm actually 965, and I have trouble with standard-sized taxis. I was wondering if you guys could give me a ride across town with one of your forklifts.

With one of our forklifts?

 Or some other heavy moving equipment.

Uh, you can't really take a forklift down the road. You don't have all the blinkers and everything else, and they sort of frown on that.

 How about a big front-end loader?

Not that I can think of. We're basically just industrial forklifts for inside use. We do get into some pneumatics that run in lumber yards, but that's not rough terrain or anything. We don't get into transporting, our equipment isn't made to run down roads with traffic involved. I'm just trying to think of where you could try that would have something that would be of that nature...

 Maybe a construction company, with heavy dump trucks. Those could go down city roads, right?

Right, exactly, they're set to go around town. They're more equipped to be able to do that.

 Well, my family is having a big family reunion soon, held outdoors at a park with a nice, level surface. Could you bring a forklift out to take me around to the different picnic tables?

Yeah, that could be possible, sure. But as far as getting you to that park, that would be a problem, as far as using my equipment.

 Oh, God, my life.

Hey, what about a flatbed trailer? You know, if you had a truck with a flatbed trailer, of course then the flatbed trailer would have blinkers and brake lights and everything.

 Hey, great idea! Do you think I should strap myself down like King Kong so I don't roll off the edge?

I don't think that's a bad idea, to at least have something to hold onto. Yeah, I think a flatbed trailer would be your best bet, because they got their own surge-brake system, they have all the lights and equipment, you could just hook it onto a pickup truck and go.

 You were talking about the pneumatic lifts that you work with before. Is that something you could install in my house, to get me out of bed and onto my flatbed trailer?

They're too industrial. I'm trying to think of the place that's down the road from us, I know they make a lot of motorized wheelchairs, and they also get into lifting on stairways, where people can sit on it and ride up and down and stuff like that.

 Maybe I could install big conveyor belts going through every room of my house. Especially the bathroom.

I'm sure you could. But if you called up an A-Z Rental or Rent-All or something like that, they've got flatbed trailers. You'd have to get somebody that could haul you... a truck or a car with a hitch, even, would work.

 Thanks for your ideas. Well, if you ever see a 965-pound man getting hauled around town on a flatbed trailer, give me a honk!

Okay, will do.

UNIVERSITY FINANCIAL AID OFFICE

 Hi, my name is Mike and I weigh over 900 pounds, so I have some disabilities as far as moving around. Does the university have any scholarships to help recruit heavier students and bring diversity to the student body?

Female Financial Aid Officer: That is a very good question. Actually, because I'm still fairly new here, it's a question that I've never been asked before, but I know that there are always initiatives to encourage diversity here on campus. That's for certain. And we really encourage students with disabilities to definitely try to participate and become a part of the university. Do you have disabilities as a result of obesity, or—

 Just the disability of being so huge that I can't walk around at all. I've been looking into different methods of transportation, though, and I think that I'll be able to rent a flatbed trailer to get around campus.

Okay, and are you a current student here?

 No, but I was hoping to study television, since that's one of the things I know best. But I would need special conditions, like having lecture seats widened for me to sit in. Could those sorts of things happen for me, making it possible for me to attend class?

Well, it depends on your personal preference, and also the nature of your program. They're actually starting a lot of distance learning, where you can take some classes here at the university and then some via the Internet. That might be something you would be interested in—not discouraging you from coming here and participating in campus life, but just as an option. And I could look into some of that information if you'd like me to.

Could you? I don't have my trailer yet to get down there.

No problem. What we can do is send you some information, but I'll also get back to you via telephone so that I can let you know what I found out. Could I get your telephone number and mailing address, Mike?

 Sure, it's *(provides information)*.

Let's see, this is your first contact with us?

 That's right.

And are you planning on enrolling in the fall of next year?

 I was hoping to, but I'm curious about those scholarships for students who are gravitationally challenged.

Okay, can you think of any other questions you might want me to investigate a little bit?

 Geez, there's the lecture seats, I would need parking space for my trailer, my dorm bed would have to be reinforced with concrete, and I could use a notetaker because writing makes me tired.

Okay...

 My fingers are too big to grip a pen, anyway.

Did you look into just the regular financial aid yet, by any chance?

 No, not yet. I was hoping to make my weight work for me.

Okay, just wanted to know if that's something you'd thought about. But I can find out about the scholarships too. It's always nice if you can get money that you don't have to pay back! *(chuckles)* Are you easy to reach at a specific time of day?

 I never leave my house.

I will do my best to try to track down someone today, and if for some reason I don't get the answers to your questions I'll call you back tomorrow or early next week. But I'm usually pretty good about getting back, so I will try to do that today or tomorrow.

Thank you so much, ma'am. I'll just lay here and wait for your call.

Okay, thank you for calling us. Bye-bye.

HOLIDAY FOOD DRIVE

 Hi, I saw your ad on television. This is the Christmastime hunger drive?

Holiday Food Drive Lady: Right, the Share Your Holidays.

 Okay, I think that I can offer something to your program. I was hoping to perform as a Santa Claus at your functions.

(near–orgasmic intake of breath) Oh, that would be so great! Yeah, our kickoff celebration—I don't know if this is too early for Santa—is tomorrow. Channel 15 is going to be here at our food bank to do the kickoff, doing a Live At Five, and also for part of the six o'clock news. And we're having some Girl Scouts come out, and the Mad Hatters, they're a singing group at the university, and the Wienermobile—

 If there's Girl Scout cookies and Oscar Mayer products, I'm there.

Yeah, it is the kickoff of a holiday thing, so I don't know if you're available tomorrow night, but that would be so great!

 Well, I think that I'm suited for the role because—

No pun intended!

 Ha ha. I weigh 965 pounds.

Oh.

 So obviously, I could do a pretty good job as Santa. Now if I help out, I don't need to be paid, but since you are a food drive, could I get some food out of the deal?

Oh, we're really strict on how we operate. We're only allowed through our national headquarters to distribute food to people at or below the poverty level. So that is not a possibility... we only give it out to people who really need it.

I really need it, ma'am.

Well, even so, we don't distribute food to individuals, you'd have to get it from a food pantry. We supply all the area food pantries and meal sites with our food. We never distribute to individuals.

Whenever I go to food pantries, it seems like the people there are scared of me.

The other thing, if Thursday doesn't work, we're also having a grand finale, this is a much bigger event, and it will be in December. It's December 9th at the County Expo Center. It starts at three or four and goes until about eight or nine, and the public comes out and donates food, and it's much more of a celebratory thing. So that might be more appropriate for Santa.

That sounds like fun. I should definitely have my trailer by then.

Yeah, so if you want to call back in a little bit, we can give you more details. Right now we're more concerned with the kickoff tomorrow, but then, like I said, December 9th is our grand finale, and it's a big celebration.

Do you know of some good pantries I could go to in the meantime to get lots and lots of free food?

Do you think that you would fall under those guidelines?

I will do whatever it takes.

Okay, different pantries have different ways of finding that information out from their clients. What I suggest you do is contact First Call For Help. They have a listing of the various pantries and their hours and locations. You could then go to whichever one is closest to you and find out what their requirements are. But I'm going to give you their number and they can give you the information on where those places would be.

I'm ready to make that call.

Okay, their number is (*provides number*).

And could I get back in touch with you as far as playing Santa a little bit later?

Sure, that would be great. Okay, I have to go now.

 All right, thanks. I'll start working on my costume here. Ho ho ho!

NASA

Female Receptionist: Good afternoon, NASA Public Affairs, may I help you please?

 Hi, my name is Mike and I'm calling because I'm a very heavy man. I weigh over 900 pounds, and I want NASA to put a zero-gravity system in my home—

Hold on, okay, you say you weigh over 900 pounds?

 Right.

Okay, and what is it that you want NASA to do?

 I have trouble moving around my home, so I thought NASA could install a zero-g system here so it's like I'm on the Space Shuttle—

Would you hold, please?

 No problem. *(on hold)*

Okay, sir.

 Okay, I'm hoping I can purchase some NASA technology to put into my home so gravity doesn't drag me down so much. I want to just float around my house and live a normal life again.

I don't know anything about that... we don't have that type of program. Have you tried other types of programs?

 The Russian space program is pretty crappy now, isn't it?

I meant weight-loss programs.

 Not as far as the gravity. It seemed like you were the ones to call on that.

I'm not sure we have anything like that.

But NASA has low-gravity training facilities for astronauts, right?

Yeah, but that would be just for astronauts, we don't have anything like that for sale. You see, we not in the market or business to sell things, we basically space-oriented. And we try to find out what's out there to help the people. But far as having equipment such as you talking about for marketing, we don't have.

 Perhaps NASA could form a partnership with a private company to market their technology. There's a lot of people out there who are tired of fighting gravity, but don't want to give up the foods they love.

I don't have the power to make that decision, sir.

 You could make a ton of money on zero-gravity home units. How about an ad campaign like "Don't Stop Bloating... Start Floating!"

Let me transfer you to another person. *(forwarded into voice mail—call is never returned)*

THE UNITED NATIONS

 Hi, this is the refugee center?

Female Representative: Yes.

 You're the people who drop food supplies over countries like Kosovo and East Timor?

Yes, sir.

 I'm here in Wisconsin and I have trouble leaving my bedroom because I weigh over 900 pounds. I was wondering if there were any flights going over the Midwest that could drop some of their food supplies near my home.

I don't think so, because these types of arrangements are made within the region. The U.N.H.C.R. has stockpiles in certain areas of the world, and the whole idea is to get it as close to the point of distribution as possible, and as far as I know, nothing flies over the continental U.S.A.

There's no hunger disasters looming on the horizon for the rural Midwest?

Not that I know of. You'd have to check with other organizations, but as far as the U.N. is concerned, I don't believe there is anything like that. This is all done within the region, as I said.

 So there's never any connecting flights going from coast-to-coast or anything?

No, no.

 I've read about the high-protein biscuits that are dropped—

Mm-hmm.

 —and they sound delicious. Could I purchase some of those from your gift shop?

Not from U.N.H.C.R. You should check with some of the major manufacturers here in the U.S.A. I don't know who they are, but I'm sure that if you have access to a computer and you went on the Internet, you could find out.

 What is the Internet?

You don't know what the Internet is?

 No, what is that?

It's the global computer network. You can go on it and look stuff up.

 Huh. Could these manufacturers super-size my protein biscuits? I think my appetite might be a little bigger than your average East Timor person.

I really don't know that information, sir.

 Okay, I'm just really hungry, and I have trouble leaving my home.

I'm sorry, I can't give you any advice other than what I've done.

 Well, thank you for telling me about that Internet thing, and keep dropping those biscuits.

Okay. Good luck, 'bye.

FAT-TRAPPING POWDER

Hi, this is Mike Loew. I've been taking your fat-trapping powder, and I've shat out almost 800 pounds!

Female Representative: Congratulations, sir.

It's an amazing product. The best thing is, I didn't have to give up my favorite foods. In fact, I'm enjoying a plate of ribs as we speak!

That's great.

It's really changed my life around. I've moved back to Los Angeles, and I won a seat on the city council! Now, I've seen your ads, where the powder binds to the bacon grease poured into a glass of water, rendering the fat undigestable.

Yes.

I want to purchase a huge quantity of your powder to put in the public water supply here. I have a proposal to get this in our water supply and make it easy for everyone in Los Angeles to lose weight—with no sweaty exercises!

What you would have to do is fax that request in, to *(provides number)*.

Okay, do they have more medical expertise there to answer my question?

You said you wanted to purchase in bulk, right?

Right.

So you would have to fax that request in to see if they could get you a wholesale price.

Great! Do you think it would work to put your powder in the water supply?

You can go ahead and put that on the fax as well. And usually if you do put it in the water, that will be fine, it should basically take no time to take effect.

 So you don't think there's any problem with mass application of your product?

You would have to fax that information and then they'll contact you regarding that. Because people shower with the water, you know, so I'm not sure how that would work.

 Okay, but is it safe for everyone to ingest? You might think that we all look good and exercise out here in L.A., but we have the same fat people that you see everywhere else.

Usually we do suggest that anybody under twelve not take it, because if they are under twelve, they really don't need to diet because their body is growing. If they are a little chubby when under twelve, then it might just be baby fat.

 I see. We do have some flabby children in the area—do you have a fat-trapping powder for kids, with a fruity flavor or something?

No, we don't have anything for the children. So, just fax that in and they will get back to you on that.

 Okay, but you think that I could buy as much powder as it takes and just put it right in the water supply?

I don't think that will be a problem, sir.

 This country rocks!

Thank you and have a great day.

Mike Loew is now once again wearing his size-32 jeans and admiring himself in front of a full-length mirror.

TELEMARKETER

Hello?

Female Telemarketer: Hello, is this Mike Loew?

Yeah.

Hi, this is Beth Schoepke, and I'm calling from U.S.A. Price Club. We'd like to give you the opportunity to receive $90 in free gas. We're conducting a market test in your area for our U.S.A. Price Club membership, and that's where you're guaranteed the best prices available for thousands of name-brand items and services that you use every day. And since this is a market test, you would receive $90 in gasoline coupons to use, as a Price Club member simply for trying the no-obligation thirty-day trial. Now as a member of U.S.A Price Club, you can enjoy exciting privileges such as credit-card registration and guaranteed big savings on travel, major appliances, prescription drugs, electronics—

One thing—I got rid of my car, so could I use the gasoline to burn things?

You could use the gasoline for anything you want, it's your gas.

All right, if you say so.

Yeah, it doesn't matter, you can save even on movie tickets, new cars, if you were to buy a car you can receive a rebate, and insurance plans, magazines, even real estate transactions as well as eyewear and contact lenses. Now, just for participating in the market test, we will send you your $90 in gasoline coupons simply for trying the no-obligation thirty-day trial membership, so I could send it out for you today at no obligation and then you can see for yourself how you would never have to pay full price again for the thousands of name-brand items and services that you use everyday. Does that sound okay?

So I could save money by buying thousands of items every day.

Mm-hmm, that's correct.

Actually, I've been trying to simplify my life lately. The gasoline is interesting though, because I've been burning a lot of my things, just to get rid of them, in the backyard. So could I just get the gas?

Well, we could send you out the membership kit, and then you would receive the gasoline coupons, the $90 in gasoline coupons are yours to keep whether you keep the membership or not, so you could try it for the thirty-day free trial period, and if you chose not to continue, you can simply call our toll-free number and cancel, and then you would not owe anything, and the gasoline coupons would be yours to keep. Now if you chose to become a member, the yearly membership fee is $89.95, but if you don't save a thousand dollars in the first year, you do receive a full refund of the membership fee.

That sounds fine, let's go ahead with that.

Okay, now I just need to verify the *(clears throat)* bank card that we have on file, and the last four numbers on that card are 4-0-2-3? Okay, and it's a MasterCard, and the expiration date is 7 of 99? Do you have a new expiration date on that?

Uh, I'm afraid I don't, actually.

You don't, it's expired? Do you have another credit card that you'd want to use then?

Let me think... oh wait, I melted down all my credit cards in a big bonfire early this morning. Can I still get that gasoline?

No, I'm afraid not. Thank you for your time, 'bye.

Use the space above to draw a picture of how Tough Call *makes you feel.*

VACATION
TIME

For two glorious weeks out of every year, American adults are released from their cubicles to scamper about freely. However, those who dare to leave the comforts of home face rude airline clerks, agonizing layover delays, foreign toilets with serious water-pressure problems, and land mines. Ignoring the risks, Mike Loew speaks to a number of travel industry professionals in his personal quest to get away from it all.

CRUISE TRAVEL AGENCY

Cruise Travel Agency: Good afternoon, Calypso Cruise Travel, this is Kip.

 Hallo, Kip. I am a German naval veteran of World War Two, and I would like to go on a fun cruise. I want a below-the-water-line cabin, as I once captained a U-boat.

Okay.

 I am looking for, how do you say it, a nostalgic getaway.

Okay, what date or what cruise line, do you have any thoughts there?

 Something cruising the North Atlantic would be delightful. Do you work with German cruise lines?

Hmm, not that I know of. I would have to dig around for some info on that. We do a lot of cruises in the Caribbean or in the Mediterranean, but North Atlantic, I'd have to look around for some info.

 Or, the North Sea, near Jutland, would also be fine.

Yeah. What dates are you thinking of?

 January.

Okay, I don't think there would be any cruises in the North Atlantic in January.

 No? I dream of bitter wind on cold steel, Kip.

Yeah, I can look and see if we have any information on that, I don't know what I might find, if anything, but I can certainly look. Why don't I get your name and number, and I can check and give you a call back.

 Yes, I am Oberleutnant zur See Michael Loew, and my number is *(provides number)*. Also, I hope to travel with a number of my old comrades from the Kriegsmarine. Do you think there would be the possibility of sharing a cabin with twenty other men?

Well, probably only two or four to a cabin, in most cases.

We would not be disruptive. We are used to very tight quarters, and worked out many ingenious systems while undersea together in the war. I hope to have at least fifteen of my men with me at all times.

Probably not in one cabin, I mean, yeah, I'm not really sure what there might be.

 Hmm. All right, if you would be so kind as to investigate German cruise lines navigating the North Atlantic in January with a below-the-water-line cabin capable of holding at least fifteen men, I would greatly appreciate it.

Okay, yeah, I can check and see what the possibilities are.

 Wonderful.

Okay, I will give you a call back this afternoon, then.

 Danke schön.

EMBASSY OF ANGOLA

 Hi, my name is Mike, and I'm a father who's hoping to take his family on a little vacation to your country soon.

Angolan Woman: Um, you are going to Angola only on vacation?

 Yeah, we were hoping to just have a nice time there and drive around, and I was curious about fun things to do in Angola.

Okay, because the situation is bad. Are you aware of the war situation in Angola?

 No!

Yah, I thought so. Because at this time, in Luanda, there is safety in the capital, but you won't be able to travel, at least by road, out of the capital town.

 Oh, what sort of problems are there?

The war has been getting worse this year.

The war? There's people fighting?

Yah, we have a civil war, because there is a fight between the government and one military group opposed to the government, the UNITA. I don't know if you've heard about that, but in this last year, the war has been increased a lot. We hope it's going to be the last war, but really the situation is very bad.

 You don't think I should pile the kids in the minivan and drive around Angola?

No no no no no, not at all, sir, not at all. No way. No way. Because outside the capital, the streets are not safe, on one hand, because there are groups around attacking, attacking cars and all the stuff. Also, because of the mining, because we didn't have all the country... de-mined, can I say that?

 Sure, go for it.

Okay, not yet, because this is a continuation of twenty years of war. Yah, I do not know if you are aware, we have a very serious situation on land mines, we are one of the first countries in the world, unfortunately, with land mines.

 Land mines? That actually explode when you step on them?

Uh-huh, we have the antipersonnel land mines especially.

 So I couldn't run around with the kids and play Frisbee?

No, I would suggest no Frisbee. I am from Angola and I am very proud of my country, but I'm trying to tell you the truth. I don't wanna just scare you, but I want to let you know exactly what you are going to find. In terms of a visa, at this moment they are not be issuing tourist visa, because of the situation, okay? We cannot assure the best security for our tourists who don't want of course that anybody gets hurt or injured or something like that down there. So, at this moment, we are not issuing tourist visa. We are, yes, issuing visas for flying people to Angola, if you're going to work or, at least, if you have someone down there that invites you. We call it a letter of invitation, and that person is going to be responsible for anything that happens to you, you know?

Okay, so I just have to make friends with some people from Angola first, and then we could go.

Yah, at this point, hopefully, if the war finish very soon, and we do really believe it's gonna be soon, it's not gonna take much longer—

Hey, that's great.

—of course, all this is gonna be revoked! *(pronounced as three syllables, rhyming with "he smoke it")* And we gonna have open again the tourist visas, and okay, we gonna send you the information on sites and places, you know?

So once the war does lift, there's places there or places that will be going up, like tourist resorts and theme parks?

Sorry sorry, I don't understand?

Oh, as soon as the war is over, there are nice places to go to?

Oh, yah, of course, we are close to the sea, we have beautiful beaches, we have a beautiful island, very very beautiful island in Luanda, okay, we have mountains, we have valleys, okay, naturally, Angola is very beautiful. We have beautiful, beautiful places, and the people there are eager, waiting for the ending of the war, in order to invest in the tourism, yes, there are going to be more and more places.

It sounds so nice, I don't know why people are so bent out of shape and fighting each other so much.

Okay, it's quite a long story, there is political reasons. What I can tell you, if you want to know a little more about Angola, you can consult our Web site, that is www.angola.org *("org" pronounced with a soft g)* and you can find some information there, if you wanna be updated about any issues.

Sure, I'll surf over there right now with my laptop and wireless modem. But do you think I should cancel my Angola travel plans for the time being, until the war wraps up?

If you are traveling with kids, and it's gonna be your first time, I don't want to tell you, but I would consider—

Yeah, I do have three small children, and they are quite a handful!

Yeah, small children, and in your case, you are an American citizen, right?

Yes.

Yah, I would consult the Department of Trade, because they have rules and information about all countries, you know, with U.S. has diplomatic relations, and they also have orientations for people, so you can hear from both sides, and I hope it's gonna help out on your decision, of course that decision is gonna be yours. But I would be more than glad to give you information any time you wish.

Well, how about those land mines? Is there anything I should look for to avoid stepping on a land mine?

Any, any place outside Luanda, especially the small village, especially the roads, especially the bridge, all these different areas, you have to be very, very aware. We are one, you can compare the statisticals, we are one of the first countries in the world with most people with amputations because of land mines. Okay, this is a very serious issue. Even late Princess Diana, she was working on that issue also, and she visited Angola, she was doing a great job on that. It's not like saying there's some mines here and some there—

People step on them everywhere?

Yah, again with statisticals, we are about eleven million habitants, and we have two-and-a-half millions per person.

You have two-and-a-half million mines per person?

No, not million mines, two-and-a-half mines per person.

Oh, two-and-a-half, okay, that's not too bad. But I will have to keep an eye on the kids. They love to run around, especially Tyler. So there's nothing I can tell the kids to watch out for?

I beg your pardon?

The land mines, they're pretty well hidden?

Yah, the problem with land mines is like this, you don't know that they are there until you step on it. You step on the ground, and the antipersonnel land mines, they are put under the ground, and they just be activated as soon as you step on it.

That sounds like a real headache.

And you don't know, because can be also small grass growing, there's nothing telling you that there is a mine there. You can put a land mine today, and they can be activated twenty years from now. This is the very danger part, there's nothing, nothing, nothing that's going to tell you there is a land mine there. Unless it is a big one, okay, like an antitank that is not going to be activated with the weight of a person. But the problem that we have is the majority of the land mines we have spreaded around the fields are antipersonnel mines. So, any kid, anything, can activate the mine.

Okay, then there's the people there, you mentioned some folks who wouldn't be so friendly to us when we're out on the road?

What I was trying to tell you is that to travel outside the town is definitely not safe. Nobody does it, not even us. We just travel by air, and only when extremely necessary. That is the real situation. Okay, because the people is friendly, but if you are attacked, and this happens every single day in every single point of the country, by a UNITA group, they're not going to let you go. They kill you.

That's not very welcoming.

Yah, okay, that is it. It's not a question of a good argumenting or something, no, no. They don't even ask you before they kill you. It is a brutal war.

Wow, what's their deal? Why would they want to kill an American?

First of all, they don't even bother to know who you are, because nowadays the guns are very sophisticated. So they don't even need to approach you, they just see a car, and you are not supposed to cross, you know? I'm deeply sorry to tell you that, sir, but I would feel bad if I lied to you. But if you go to the capital, okay, the capital is safe, the only problem you have in the capital is in some neighborhoods, like anyplace else, okay, in some neighborhoods it's not very good to go, especially at night, stuff like that. But only the capital. And because of this war situation, the capital has one problem, that it's overpopulated now. And you have, this is not for scaring you, it's normal and you can be there and nothing happens, but you have to be aware of pickpockets, this kind of stuff. But I'm not telling you they're going to kill you, no no no no no, it's different stuff.

 So are there plans, when the war is all wrapped up, for setting up some nice golf courses and water parks where all those war refugees could get jobs selling hot dogs?

Yah, but the majority of parks are closed because of this situation. There is a big park where you can see the animals, that was beautiful, but at this time, since last year, it's closed too, because you have to travel. It's about one-and-a-half hours from Luanda. Now, it is no longer safe. Many animals were killed. There are troops patrolling, but it's no longer safe. But, the good news is, we really, really believe that the war is finally now at the end. This is one of the more crucial points, but we do believe that it is going to be our last sacrifice.

 That's great, because my wife has really been bugging me to take her to Angola. Will there be an agreement reached between the two sides, or is one side going to lose?

No, unfortunately not. We have been doing agreements, especially in the past six years, but the opposite group has been breaking all the agreements.

 So the plan now is to crush them?

That's what the government decided, okay, it's cost too much life, it's cost too much to the economy, to the country, to the everywhere, so it is going to be the last war. And they don't respect anything, they don't respect human life, I mean, nothing at all! The problem is not the other movement, it's okay, sometimes it's good to have opposite leaders, it helps you out to watch yourself, but the problem is with the leader of that movement—the man is completely crazy. And he wants the power at all costs, and he wants the power just because he wants the revenge, and because of that, he was proclaimed a criminal of war. A very very strong section agreed, many many countries in Europe are against him, and now this war is about searching for him. We are trying to captivate him, okay, and put an end to this.

 Well, Angola certainly has captivated me. I can put off the trip for a little while, but hopefully before too long we will fly there to see your beautiful mountains and valleys.

Definitely, and I do believe that we can do that trip quite shortly.

 Great. Thanks so much for all your information and all your honesty.

Oh, I thank you, sir, and thank you for being interested in our country. And I wish you a very merry Christmas.

 I wish the same to you, ma'am, and I also wish you and your people all the best in crushing your hated ethnic rivals.

Oh, thank you so much. Good-bye.

DOG KENNEL

 Hi, I'm calling because my wife and I will be going on a vacation soon, and I was wondering if I could store my kids there at your kennel.

Female Kennel Owner: What days are you looking for?

 We're going to be gone from December 29th to January 20th.

Gosh, I'm sorry, I'm booked for New Year's... *(sound of dogs barking)* I'm sorry, you said January 29th, or December?

 December 29th to the middle of January.

Yes, right now I am full for those days. I could take your name and number, and then if something becomes available, I could give you a call.

 Okay, I appreciate that. My name is Mike Loew—

Have you boarded or groomed with us in the past?

 No, I haven't. But do you think you could take care of my kids?

If I get some changes here. Uh, the Rose Bowl really took care of New Year's, but you never know. It was Mike Loew?

 Yeah, and my phone number is *(provides number).*

And is that two dogs?

Two kids.

And would they be able to share a run or would you need separate kennels?

 Oh, I think they could share.

And we have no problem with that as long as there's no arguing over food or feeding problems.

 Yeah, they get along pretty well together.

Okay!

 Do you have a television or something for them to watch?

Uh, we have a radio.

 Do you have board games?

Are you talking about real children or dogs?

 Oh, real children.

We're a boarding facility for dogs.

 Right. I was just thinking about kennels that I've seen in the past, and they seem to have some water and some food out there and a little space to run around, so I just thought I'd stow the children there for a couple of weeks. We're having trouble finding a baby-sitter for the millennium.

Oh, okay, well I'm sorry, we don't take the two-legged type.

 You don't?

No. We strictly board four-legged dogs.

 Do you think that you could make an exception?

I don't think so.

 The kids could probably have fun with the dogs, running around with them and stuff.

I bet you they would.

 Okay then, we're all set.

No, I'm sorry, I can't help you with that.

 They're good kids, they wouldn't give you much trouble, I don't think.

I'm sure they wouldn't.

 But you don't have space for them?

Nope.

 Well, if something opens up, you can give me a call back.

Uh, you know, I just doubt it. I'm sorry I couldn't be of help to you.

 Hey, don't beat yourself up. You're only sending my children off to Angola to step on a landmine.

This chapter is not intended for use as an actual travel guide, since the foreign conditions reported may not be accurate after press time. Therefore, Mike Loew cannot assume any liability if the world becomes an increasingly weird place.

TOBACCONIST'S

 Hi, this is Mike from Los Angeles. I've been smoking for a couple of months now, but I'm having trouble getting hooked on the cigarettes. They make my throat and lungs hurt, they make me cough, and I was wondering if you had any tips to help me be a better smoker.

Tobacconist: Eww, well, what kind of cigarettes are you smoking?

 Camel Lights, Marlboro Reds, that kind of stuff.

Okay, so you're smoking a lot of domestic cigarettes, huh?

 I'm doing my best.

Best thing I could suggest to you, Mike, is come in, let us roll you a couple of 100 percent natural tobacco cigarettes. That's what we focus on here. We don't sell domestic cigarettes in here, we sell imported cigarettes from England, Switzerland, Germany, Canada, some high-end American cigarettes, but none with the additives you get across the counter in the U.S. And I think that you might get real tobacco taste by trying some of the products we sell. Now I can't, you know, *(chuckles)* everybody's physiology is a little different, but if you're looking to continue trying to smoke, and looking for something better, I think this is a stop you must make if you want to continue. We'll show you fifteen different kinds of unadulterated tobacco.

 So the Europeans make a smoother, more suave cigarette?

This is my philosophy—because Europe is so socialized, the government pays for all the health care, and if they're going to sell something in their countries, they're going to make it as clean as possible. That's what the European market is known for, and that's what the U.S. market is really starting to gain. Our bulk cigarette and tobacco sales have tripled in the last six months.

 Good for you. Is that all on the strength of your fancy smokes?

That's right, because we offer the quality. So come on in, let us roll you a couple, give us a half-hour, smoke a couple, and see if what I'm saying comes into place for your health. Okay?

Is the natural tobacco a healthier smoke than the commercial brands?

Well, there's no additives put into it. And I'm someone who really believes that there's over 600 additives in domestic cigarettes, and that's what they're trying to hide.

 What do they hide in there?

Saltpeter to sulfur. Lots of different things. They don't want you to smoke it for enjoyment, they want you to smoke it to get to your next one. And if you smoke a couple of these—we've even had comments that people have cut down their smoking since they started to roll their own.

 Oh, I don't want to cut down. I want to continue to smoke because I like the way it looks—everybody thinks I'm really cool when I light up—but I'm just trying to make it a little easier on myself.

That's what you're looking for, but we're more into the taste and the quality of the tobacco. But that might come hand-in-hand with the look you're going for.

 So the taste that you guys offer is richer, more flavorful—

Very different, and clean. I think I'll leave it at that. Very clean.

 That sounds refreshing. I wish I could be a rugged, dirty smoker like the Marlboro Man, but I guess I'm not.

Tell you what, I bet that after we roll you a few, you won't ever want to smoke a Marlboro again.

 Well, I still have a pack to finish off here, so do you have any smoking techniques I could try in the meantime?

If I were you, I would work on your rolling technique, okay? Roll your own and discover the taste of 100 percent natural tobacco.

 Okay. Thanks for the wise words, sir. I'm just a young smoker, and I need all the guidance I can get.

You bet. Thanks for calling, and I hope we see you in here soon!

READY TO
ROCK

Dazzling new recording techniques, the global reach of MTV, and a mass audience with increasing disposable income and decreasing taste—all of these factors have made it easier than ever to become a rock star. Yet for some reason, Mike Loew has still not sung his heart out to a crowd of fifty thousand shrieking teenage girls. As a living example for those who share similar aspirations, Loew attempts to break into the music industry the only way he knows how—with white-hot rock and roll passion.

DRUMMER WANTED

 Hey bro, this is Mike from Los Angeles. How's it hangin'? I saw your ad in *Metal Monthly* about how you're looking for a drummer.

Guy Who Wants Drummer: Yup.

 Well, look no further. I'm totally into your favorite bands—Rush, Megadeth, Iron Maiden—that you've got here. I own an awesome top-of-the-line drum kit with twelve tom-toms, I've got about fifteen cymbals, I have a van to cruise around in, all that stuff.

Wow, great. Do you have a good space to practice in?

 Yeah, I was in this band before, so I've got a secure practice space. First floor, easy to load into... it's sweet, dude.

Sounds pretty good!

 Plus, I can throw my drumsticks way up in the air and catch them nine times out of ten.

Okay, well, here's what we've got right now. Myself and the singer basically are starting this up. So we want to get together with our potential drummers and then start auditioning other people, because we have three possible guitarists for a second guitar. We got one call from a bass player but he never called me back and didn't leave a number, so we still don't have bass, but that's what we have so far.

 Okay, let me tell you about my history. I consider myself a pretty hot drummer and I've been playing out for years now. The one problem is that I was kicked out of my last band because I got all the chicks. I don't know if it's the hair or the tight pants that I wear or what, but the chicks go nuts for me. So I don't know if that's going to bother you guys...

All right, we'll see how it goes.

 Hey, I can guarantee that's the way it will go with me around. What do you think?

Well, I think we should definitely get together and see what we can figure out. Right now I don't have an actual amp up here, I just got a four-by-twelve ordered, but I'll probably start out by just bringing my little Marshall combo, which is good enough to just, you know, try things out. So I'm thinking probably this weekend, I'm going to be bringing that up, and once I have that up here, we can get together and jam a little bit or something.

 Okay. Do you guys plan on doing shows with a lot of chicks at them?

Uh, we hope so.

 That might be a problem, because it did become a problem with the other guys I was jamming with. I would always cruise in there and leave with all the chicks.

You're that much of a thing?

 I've got the drumstick-twirling down, I've got the long, frosted hair— I've got real style. It's been my experience that the ladies can't get enough of me, and I can understand how other rockers would start feeling bad about themselves—but what can I do?

I don't know, we'll have to see. Yeah, I don't know if that's going to be a problem or not. I mean, we're definitely looking to get some chicks, that's one thing we have agreed on.

 So along with the music, you're dedicated to scoring some chicks.

Yeah. We're both working on the hair, but my friend is a little ahead of me—

 Do you guys do anything with it?

What, with the hair?

 Yeah, are you teasing it out, are you frosting it, perming it—

Nah, it's pretty much just a long kind of thing. I don't have long hair yet, just to warn you. I have been working on it, but it's going to take a while. I basically decided a couple of months ago—I'm a freshman here at the university—I decided around February, I'm going to grow my hair.

 Well, the bands that you have here—Megadeth, Dream Theater— those bands had some great hair, if that's the kind of look we're going for.

We're probably going in the direction of Dream Theater, where they have hair but they don't really do anything crazy with it. But, it sounds like you have what we're looking for, if you're into all those bands, and you have gear, and a van. Space was something that I was worried about, since I just bought a four-by-twelve. I was hoping to leave my half-stack somewhere, since I can't really drag it back and forth to my dorm room. But the combo would be easier to bring over and just try out some songs.

 And if the whole chick thing doesn't bother you too much, it certainly doesn't bother me. Maybe I could even teach you guys a thing or two.

I can't say for sure whether or not it will bother us. Coincidentally, I mentioned it to my singer online here, because I'm online with him right now, and he says it doesn't bother him.

 Do you guys ever talk to chicks on the Internet?

Once in a while. Yeah, it doesn't bother him, so I'm sure we'll figure something out.

 Well, if he's the vocalist, I'm sure he's thinking about his lyrics and song-crafting instead of the chicks.

Well, he thinks about chicks plenty, too. And I'm working on getting a good guitar act down. I have a lot of influence from all the guitar heroes of the past.

 Excellent. Do you have any stage outfits together?

Nothing special right now, other than what we wear.

 Are you into skin-tight zebra-print pants?

I don't know how far we would go. Right now, on a day to day basis, we're into the black jeans, black band T-shirt thing.

 I have a couple of extra pairs of animal-print Spandex tights if you guys want to borrow them.

I would have to discuss that with the singer. We do want good stage presence, and want to put on a good performance, not just stand there and play. We want to reach out and grab the audience, but I don't know if we're going to incorporate a lot of outfits into it. I like what Dream Theater and Queensryche do, where they're not doing the whole Spandex thing, but they still have interesting outfits.

 Can I still wear my zebra pants?

I guess so. I mean, you're behind the drums, right?

 That doesn't matter. The floor of the club will still be sopping wet, and not with beer. Okay, let's make a practice schedule, dude.

RURAL SCHOOL SUPERINTENDENT

 Hi, my name is Mike Loew, and I have a son who's enrolled in your school district. I'm wondering what sort of programs are available there for children to learn rhyming skills.

Female Superintendent: To learn rhyming skills... What grade is your son in?

 He's in second grade. My rhyming career isn't going anywhere fast, but I do have high hopes for my son.

Okay, our reading program has a phonics component, and our spelling program has a phonics component, which would focus on rhyming. For example, you would be looking for words that have the long "a" vowel sound, and that would be one way to teach rhyming. Poetry, of course, incorporates rhyming, and there would be units taught where kids are actually writing poetry. Are you thinking about rhyming skills in terms of helping your son with language development, or is it for another reason?

 Well, I've read in *People* magazine how we're increasingly becoming a hip-hop culture. Naturally, I want my child to be able to really rip it on the microphone, so he can compete in the rap battles of the future. Do you have rappers coming in to do affirmative action programs for Caucasian children, to learn hip-hop rhyming skills?

Oh, I don't know what hip-hop is. I know what rap is.

 Hip-hop is the whole culture, and rap is it's music. It all started with the release of the Sugar Hill Gang's hit single "Rapper's Delight" back in—

What school does your son go to?

Well, I'm not sure if I want to point him out so much, because I don't want him to feel like he can't rock the party by himself.

Oh, no, I was just thinking of a way to refer you to somebody in the school, because if there's a particular interest, then teachers will try to work with parents to meet that particular interest. But the only thing based on what I know about our instructional program, we certainly don't have anything that's teaching kids how to rap. The only thing that may happen is they may, in our music program, they may focus on different types of cultures, they may teach kids different types of songs.

Something like "You Don't Want To Fuck With Me" by Ol' Dirty Bastard?

Well, I'm not so sure about that one. So it's not so much speech development, but you're talking more about singing and rapping, is that what you're more interested in?

That's right, so he'll be able to compete as he gets older with other MCs—

With other what?

MCs, you know, other rappers.

Okay. Is he interested in music, or does he have talent in that area?

Yes, he can come with the mad lyrical flow.

Okay, because we do have a talented and gifted program, and our music teachers are always trying to look at way to motivate and encourage kids, so based on what you've said so far, I think a call to the music teacher or a meeting with the music teacher, just to explain what you're interested in, and if they see any way to incorporate that. Let's see, at Franklin Elementary, the music teacher is Susan Zemelman—

Yeah, Susan Zemelman is the bomb, I could call her.

Okay, something unique about the Franklin program is that every year they put on an all-school theatrical musical, where there's acting and music. Susan always tries to get something unusual each year. I would think just a discussion about what you're interested in may get her to think about different shows that she might like to do.

And she gets the whole student body involved.

Maybe my son could get all the students to wave their hands in the air. You know, as if they just didn't care.

Sure, and the other thing is, I don't know if you have a good relationship with your son's classroom teacher, but that certainly is another opportunity, and you could talk about a variety of different things. I mean, your son only has about a month under his belt of school, and I don't know if you've had a conversation with the teacher or not, but the more conversations the parents and teachers have, the better off we all are.

Word up. Okay, I will give talk to those teachers about Tyler's rapping career. Thanks, I have to get back to work.

RANDOM HOME NUMBER

Hello, Gladys Nelson?

Gladys Nelson: Yes?

This is Mic Lo, a dope MC from Hip-Hop-Hello Phone Entertainment Services. We're the good-time rapping people.

What are you selling?

We're not selling anything to you, ma'am. A good friend of yours, who knows all about your love of hip-hop music, has arranged for you to receive a complimentary rap-o-gram from us.

A complimentary what?

An original, freestyle rap, composed for you on the spot. Now I already know your first name, so all you have to do is tell me a hobby of yours.

And this doesn't cost anything?

It doesn't cost you anything, ma'am. And my rhymes are guaranteed fresh.

All right. Well, I enjoy doing crochet. That's a hobby of mine.

Great! And heeeeere we go! Who's the boss / of hook-stitch and cross / not Tony Danza, he be makin' pasta sauce / it's Gladys / with the crazy crochet apparatus / knit it up nice like a DNA lattice / yeah she got status but not no swelled head, she / too busy making comforters for the bed, we / gotta give thanks and praise to the fingers / makin' warm little hats for all the rhyme slingers / while we spinnin' our yarns, she be spinnin' em too / bringing brothers together / Blood red and Crip blue / got the flu? / get cozy all up in her afghan / other sucka's crochet make me laugh, man / Gladys, you the phattest, don't stop your crochet / Take it to the top cuz that's what Mic Lo say... peace. Okay, there's your complimentary rap-o-gram. What do you think? Hello? Hello? (silence on other end of line) Aw, man, I can't believe she hung up. That was tight.

GERMAN EMBASSY

 Hi, this is Mike from Destiny's Labyrinth. We're a ferocious American metal band with a unique blend of speed, grace, and power, but we're having trouble becoming successful, for some reason.

Female Receptionist: And how can we help you?

 We have too much competition here in the States, but we were thinking that we could make it big in Germany, because you guys like the most ridiculous musicians over there.

I am sorry, I don't think I understand.

 You know, isn't David Hasselhoff like Elvis in your country? And I know the Backstreet Boys got their start over there too, and now they're huge. We don't wear matching pastel sweaters, though. We rock hard.

Okay, but I don't know how I can help you.

 Don't you have a Minister of Rock or something? We need to talk to someone about setting up a big concert tour in Germany.

Oh, ja, okay, but I do not have the information here. I have not lived in Germany for eight years now, so I cannot tell you how to do that, or where to go to have a concert, because I'm not sure if all the places are still there, you understand? So you would have to call the

American Embassy in Germany.

 That's a long distance call. I'd have to clear that with the guys, that could seriously cut into our beer money.

That is your decision, but that is what you must do. And I can give you that number, which is (*provides number*). All right?

 Hey, thanks. I guess I could call, but practices would really suck this week if we can't get our case of Busch Lite. But like I said, we are so ready to take over Europe. Doesn't Germany want to be a part of that?

I'm sure they would enjoy that.

BAD BOY ENTERTAINMENT

Answering Machine: Thank you for calling Bad Boy Entertainment. We are located at 1540 Broadway, on the 30th floor, New York, New York, 10036. Our fax number is (212) 381-1599. After the tone, please state the name of the person or department you're calling for, a brief message, and a phone number, including area code, where you can be reached at. Someone will return your call as soon as possible. Thank you.

 Yo, this is M-I-K-E to the L-O, calling to say hello, to the mic I'm like Yo Yo Ma to the cello, yaknowhatimsaying? This message is for Puff Daddy. Puffy, I know you're really busy wearing your white silk suits and spinning around in circles in front of your private jet, but I do hope that you have time to call me back because I want to have a rhyme battle with your sorry ass. You know, I'm a young MC ready to bring the verbal assault, Puffy's just a pebble and I'm a catapault, yeah, comin' up quick, his career's headin' south, so let me at that big-tooth sucka who can't close his mouth. My number is (*provides number*), so call back promptly to get lyrically stomped, G.

APPLEBEE'S NEIGHBORHOOD GRILL & BAR

Hostess: Hi, thanks for calling Applebee's, this is Melinda, can I make you my neighbor?

I don't know, I might keep you up all night with my rocking.

Excuse me?

 This is Mike Loew, and I'm the drummer/lead singer of an awesome metal band named Destiny's Labyrinth. I'm calling because we really need a gig tonight, and I was wondering if you guys would be okay with us coming down and jamming at your bar.

We're like a restaurant.

 Yeah, but you sell those Mucho Margaritas, so you have a bar area, right?

Yes, but we—

 Because this band seriously kicks ass, and we are so ready to rock tonight.

Okay, why don't you hold on.

(on hold)

Applebee's Manager: Hi, this is Don, can I help you?

 Hi, this is Mike Loew from Destiny's Labyrinth, a young, hungry metal band that is just starting to come up in the area. We really need a fast gig, so can we play tonight at your restaurant?

Uh, Applebee's? We don't really have a stage or anything like that. You ever been to a Bennigan's, or maybe a T.G.I. Friday's or anything like that?

 Yeah, those places rule.

We're basically that kind of restaurant, we don't have a stage or anything like that.

 I noticed that you're a neighborhood grill and bar, and we just wanted to wake up the neighborhood with our thunderous metal.

Yeah, basically what it is, we have dining with servers around in a circle around the actual area, and then we have bar dining, with a bar in the middle. It's not like a stage or a tavern or anything like that.

So you don't think that you'd have room for an eight-piece metal band?

No, we wouldn't. Okay?

 Do you know of any other good clubs in the area where we would be able to get a gig?

To be honest, I'm from Michigan. I just moved here about a month ago and I don't know the area that well, so I really wouldn't.

 So you're, like, on tour with Applebee's.

Yes, but I will probably be here for a while.

 Do you want to hear some of my lyrics? *(singing)* **Thunderous mayhem, the hammer of THOR! Eternal fire of the huge dinoSAUR! aaaaaa-AAAAAAAAAAAA—**

Sir? Sir, please stop. Thank you. I'm sorry, we just can't have that kind of music here.

 Hey, don't even try to censor us, man! We'll just come back stronger! *(pause)* So do you still have that Santa Fe Chicken Salad for $6.99?

Yes, we do, and Wednesday is our dollar-off fajita night.

 Excellent.

Mike Loew definitely thinks that you and him should get together and jam some time.

CONCRETE COMPANY

 Hi, could you guys come out here and pour some concrete? I live right next to this wetland, and it's really swampy, it has mosquitoes, and all these endangered waterfowl that make a big mess on my patio. I was hoping that you guys could just pave it over.

Female Concrete Professional: Okay, we pump concrete, but usually we have a contractor that we go through. We don't form, we just pump it. But, ya know, if you can form it up yourself, you can do it yourself.

 Oh, I would just have to build a frame for you to fill?

Yeah, the size of your slab, to hold the concrete and retain it. We don't finish it, we don't sell concrete, and we don't do forms.

 You just pump it in there.

We just pump it in there, that's all we do, all day long.

 Sounds like fun. From your ad in the Yellow Pages here, it looks like you've got some nice, big pumps.

Oh yeah.

 So that wouldn't be a problem to pave over this stinky wetland? How do I frame up my slab? Should I use some 2 x 4 lumber?

I don't know, see, I'm not a contractor. I really couldn't tell ya. My husband could probably tell ya, um, you'd have to have it plumb and all that stuff, ya kind of got to know what you're doing. That's why we usually deal with contractors. I really couldn't tell ya how to do it.

 Should I just call up a building contractor?

Yeah, what area are you in?

 Right next to the Pheasant Lake State Wildlife Area.

Okay, you could try Feist Foundation... *(speaking to someone else in her office)* Who else over there could he try? He wants to do a field-form, he wants to do a patio off the back of his house... J&M Concrete.

 J&M Concrete...

R&M Concrete. Oh, T&F Concrete. We're just pulling some contractors over there out of our heads. We can't think of anymore right offhand, but if they can't help ya, then give us a call back and we'll pull some more for ya.

Okay, so basically I get that frame ready, and then you roll over and pump it in there.

Yeah, they'll form it up for you, they'll finish it for you, they'll make sure everything's right, they might even see a way where you might not even need us. They might be able to look at your lot, and say "Oh yeah, we can get a Ready-Mix truck back here, and we won't even need those guys." And that would save you a couple dollars.

Hey, great. You're really a selfless promoter for the concrete cause.

Yeah, they could tell you if they could get in there or not, and then make sure it's done right.

Okay, I will get that frame ready, and then give you guys a call back if I need you to pump a really big load on this fragile ecosystem.

Okay!

Thanks a lot.

You're welcome! Bye-bye.

I AM
OUTRAGED

Mike Loew is widely known as a seasoned reporter—cool, observant, and unbiased. However, from time to time, he still can get his panties all in a bundle. In certain cases, this condition becomes so intense that Loew is driven to speak with the humans that have tested his patience.

CANDY KITCHEN

Hi, I just bought a big sampler of chocolates from your store—

Candy Kitchen Lady: (loudly) Right?

—and I'm pretty displeased with them, actually.

WHY?!?

Well, the—

You mean the ASSORTMENT in the BOX?

Well, they're not marked at all, I'm looking at the candies, I can't tell what's a cream, what's a nut—

The cream ones are the round ones. Yeah, the chocolate has the C, the vanilla has the V, the maple has an M, the pineapple has a P, and, uh, the black walnut we only have an X on it, that's hard to make a B as they coming out, you can't keep up.

I don't have time to figure out complex codes! What you should do is—

Well you know what? We've been doing it for seventy-five-and-a-half years just like that! We don't have a label in the box that tells you what all of them are, because it's all handmade here. Everything is handmade. And the rectangular ones are nougatines, and the round ones are badgerbacks, the square ones are caramels, um, there's some honeycomb chips in there. What else, oh and all the chocolate nuts, which is cashews, almonds, brazils, pecans and filberts.

Hmm, okay, I guess I can figure it out as I go along, but I do think you should insert an informative brochure.

Not after seventy-five-and-a-half years, we're almost finished! Ha ha.

You're almost finished? Are you being driven out by e-candy?

It's a lot of things. Yup, we've been here a long time. I'm not starting all over again. Well, I hope you enjoy it.

BATHTUB GLAZING COMPANY

 Hi, Tub Magic?

Female Receptionist: Tub Magic, uh-huh!

 I was curious about your name. I'm a little concerned—are you guys involved with the occult at all, or black magic or anything like that?

We do bathtub magic.

 It just seems to be promoting the wrong idea, like you're performing arcane rituals in the tub, and I don't think that's very Christian—

I don't have any idea what you're talking about, sir, it's just the name of a business that reglazes tubs.

 So you're not involved with any devil worship? Because I have a bathtub that needs refinishing, but I'm just concerned about your name.

I don't have any idea what you're talking about, sir, but I don't think we'd be able to help you. We are all Christians as well! *(she hangs up)*

GRAPE NUTS CEREAL 1-800 LINE

Female Grape Nuts Representative: Hello, this call may be recorded for quality purposes to better assist you. May I have your first and last name, please?

 Sure, first name Mike, last name Loew.

And how may I help you today?

 Well, I have some Grape Nuts here that I was trying to eat, and I noticed how the slogan is "Energy For Living," but I really felt very nonenergetic after I ate them. Actually, they made me feel kind of sad, just the bland taste and the endless chewing. I had to chew them for so long. I feel really depressed after eating them.

Oh, really?

 Almost suicidal, actually. The "Energy For Living" slogan just seems like a cruel joke here.

So would you like me to suggest that they change the slogan on the box?

 That might work. Something like, "Don't Eat These If You Don't Want To Feel Really Sad."

You have got to be joking me, right?

 No, ma'am. I've been staring into this bowl of drab, brown paste for two hours now. This cereal just tired me out and made me feel exhausted.

(in a sing-song voice) Well some people really love Grape Nuts, and they like them because they're so crunchy and hard! And they have a lot of vitamins and minerals in them! They're very good for you.

 Really? You sound pretty happy. Are you eating Grape Nuts?

(laughs) No, I'm eating chocolate. Actually, Hershey's Whatchamacallit. And you said that they were just too hard, and you didn't like—

 Yeah, I was just sitting there for so long, it took me so long to get going, and I just realized how long it takes to get everything done in this life. I chewed and chewed, but it seemed like I wasn't getting anywhere.

Is this the first time that you've ever tried the product?

 Yeah.

Really? Well, I'm sorry to hear that you had that unfortunate experience with our product. What kind of cereals do you like?

 I go for the healthier cereals, so I thought I'd like the Grape Nuts because they seemed natural and unsweetened. But as I said, the actual eating of them was really depressing, and to make things even worse, now they're stuck in my teeth, so I have to carry this awful memory with me all day. It's just an overwhelming breakfast product, I didn't realize what I was up against here.

Really? Well, what I can do is forward your comments up to the appropriate parties and I'm sure that if we get enough consumer response they can do something about that.

Okay.

Is there anything else that I can help you with today?

Do you have any funny stories or anything that could cheer me up?

Um, not really.

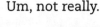

No jokes or anything?

No. All right, thanks for calling Post and you have a nice day.

I'll try. I'll try.

Good-bye.

HOSPITAL

Hi, I was born at your hospital back in 1973, and I'm pleased about that, but I'm calling because I discovered recently that I was circumcised at your hospital shortly after I was born, and I'm pretty angry about this.

Female Receptionist: Ohhh, okay. So what you need?

Well, who did this? I mean, I am just outraged that a chunk of my penis was chopped off shortly after I was born.

Mm-hmm.

Do you know who authorized this?

Okay, what I could do is transfer you to Medical Records. Maybe they will tell you what doctor circumcised you and everything. Okay?

Fine, thanks.

(on hold)

Different Woman: Medical Records, could you please hold?

Okay.

(on hold—Mike Loew drinks some water)

Hello?

 Hi, I was born at your hospital, and that went okay and everything, but I found out recently that I was circumcised there as well. I also recently discovered what circumcision is all about, so I am pretty outraged about this. I was wondering why you would do something like that.

Sir. They does that to all boys.

 Okay, but—

That came from a request from your mother, sir.

 Whoah.

And we have nothing to do with that, so you might have to talk to your mother about that, but they usually do all boys like that.

 My mom authorized this?

It would have to be your mother, sir.

 My own mother? Oh, that is hard to take. Well, do you still have my foreskin? Do you keep those?

Sir. I work in Medical Records, I wouldn't know nothing about that! (*laughs*) Bye-bye.

 Hold on, hold on. I mean, you can understand why I would be outraged at this, I mean, a decision made about my body without my con—

Well your mother made that decision for you, sir. So you have to talk to your mother about that. Okay?

 Okay, I guess I'll do that.

Okay. Bye-bye.

MY MOM

 Hi, Mom. This is Mike.

Mom: Well, Mike! How are you doing, sweetie?

 Oh, I'm okay.

Are you surviving all this working?

 Yeah, I'm fine. Just pushing ahead here.

(aside to Dad) It's Michael. What did you have on your mind?

 Oh, not much, but I was thinking about my circumcision, and I called up the hospital where I was born to ask them how that happened, and they told me that it would have had to be you that decided that. So I was outraged about that.

Are you taping this for your book? Are you, Michael? I think Michael's trying to get me in his book, Jim. Is that what you're doing? Here comes your father.

Dad: Hello?

 Hey, Dad.

Mom: Pull this on your Dad now. Now what were you concerned about, Michael?

 I'm concerned because I called up the hospital where I was born, and basically I just discovered that I was circumcised there shortly after I was born, and I was upset about that. So I wanted to call you guys and see if you still had my foreskin by any chance.

Dad: Well, no...

Mom: Oh, Michael!

Dad: Actually, we never had it, it was disposed of by the doctor. He added it to his collection.

Mom: He might be taping this for his book, Jim.

Dad: Uh-oh.

But I was just wondering what you guys were thinking back when you decided to have that done.

Dad: That was twenty-six years ago! What do you think I am, a genius?

Mom: The doctors made us do it.

Dad: Everybody did it.

 Oh, that's a good reason.

Mom: It was considered the healthy thing to do.

Dad: They didn't even talk about it. I mean, it was just done. You got your baby, two days later you take your baby home and the baby was circumcised.

Mom: I think we probably had to sign a form, Jim.

Dad: Oh, yeah.

Mom: But it was what everybody did because it was considered the healthy thing to do. Yeah, to prevent infections or something, Jim, is that what it's all about?

Dad: Something like that. You know, people that haven't been circumcised have more urinary tract infections, that type of thing. Nowadays it's a little more optional, but back then, everybody did it. Plus, it was included in the cost, so we wanted to get our money's worth.

Mom: Are you feeling sad about this, Michael?

 Yeah, I was feeling kind of sad about this, just thinking about how it was something that happened without my decision, and I've been doing some reading lately about how it compromises your sexual functioning.

Dad: No, I don't think so. Joe McCormick, whose mother was Katherine McCormick, who was a friend of my mother's, he had to have an adult circumcision, and it was extremely painful, apparently.

 I could see that.

Dad: So it's not something that you'd want to do when you're an adult.

 I'm sure that it's painful when you're a baby and you have it done, too.

Dad: They numb the appendage there.

 Oh, they do? I thought it was done without any anaesthetic.

Dad: No, they put a painkiller on there.

Mom: We were not in the room. I'm sure that if we were in the room, we would have rushed to your defense.

 Thanks. I just wonder if this made me all weird or something. Like, I was just born and suddenly I'm strapped down and the first experience of my life is getting half of my penis chopped off.

Dad: You could use that as an excuse if you needed one, I suppose.

Mom: I'm so sorry, Michael. We were young and innocent. We didn't know the ramifications of all this. We didn't know you'd call in your twenties and ask about this.

Dad: I think that in one of my boxes of old documents I have my doctor's bill, and I think they charged two dollars for it—

 Two dollars is all my foreskin's worth?!?

Dad: No, for doing it on me.

 Oh, for you. That's fine, then.

Mom: You were probably more expensive, sweetie.

Dad: My mother stayed in the hospital for a week and I think it was fifty dollars. Six dollars a day or something like that.

Mom: We've always done exactly what we thought was the best thing for you, you know, the Catholic education and all that. At the time we thought it was the right thing to do.

 Yeah, that was a lot of fun.

Mom: We had the best intentions.

I guess I can get along without the foreskin, but I was just feeling a little empty. It's something that I'll never have. I wonder what I'm missing out on.

Dad: Well, I don't know of anybody that has one, otherwise I could let you give them a call and you could ask them.

 Could you ask some of the guys at work if they have foreskins?

Dad: Well, I'm not in the habit of knowing what's inside a person's shorts.

Mom: Oh, what if my mother reads this book? She's not going to approve. So can you still come home for Christmas?

 I think so. Sure.

Mom: Do you also have to do the entire *Onion* book?

 Yeah.

Mom: How many hundreds of pages is that?

 I don't know, I'll be okay. I just gotta do the graphics.

Mom: Well, you have to pick up your brother at the airport on Thursday night, and then you can't stay up all night talking, you have to go right to bed, because you have to come up as fast as you can on Christmas Eve. That's our celebration, we're going to have dinner for you and everything. Something to make up for our transgressions, so you won't be mad at us for all your life.

 Oh, I'm not really mad, I'm just outraged. Well, I guess everyone just did it, huh?

Mom: It was just the thing to do, yup.

Dad: I don't think it was even mentioned or anything, it was just sort of done. I guess we had to sign the form for it.

 There is that.

Dad: There have been some cases where the little kid gets his little thing there burned off.

Mom: Ooh!

Dad: We were worried about that, a little bit.

 So you opted for the soft, gentle, razor blade approach instead of the inhumane burning process?

Dad: Right.

 It just seems like a strange sociocultural thing to do to little boys, the first thing you do is you chop off the most sensitive part of their body. The message seems to be "Your body is disposable, and if we go to war, the rest of your body gets thrown away, too." But anyway, are you making those chocolate-crinkle cookies again this year, Mom?

Mom: You betcha!

Dad: It's just kind of done, in Western cultures. It's Judeo-Christian in nature. We were just keeping the covenant, I guess, weren't we, Mary?

Mom: I think that was it.

 I was reading about a guy that got a circumcision as an adult, and he said that when he was having sex before, if that was a ten, now he's lucky if he gets up to two, maybe three, just because he lost so much sensitivity. So that's kind of a bummer, but hey, I'm too busy writing to think about that stuff anyway.

Mom: Who has time? Goodness.

Dad: It's something that I don't want to discuss with you in any great depth with your mother on the phone.

Mom: Would you like me to get off the phone?

Dad: Well, no, I want you to stay on the phone, actually.

 Okay, thanks for sharing, guys, I gotta go. I'm going to try to regenerate my foreskin here with some weights and pulleys. Love ya!

If anyone out there has an extra foreskin they could spare, please send it to Mike Loew in care of St. Martin's Press.

FUNERAL HOME

Hello, this is Mike Loew, and I'm calling from Los Angeles! I'm with Galactic Pictures, and we're going to be filming a big-budget movie in the Midwest this summer. I was doing some scouting here, and I noticed your ad says "Known For Our Lifelike Preservation." I was wondering if we could possibly do some shooting on the grounds of your funeral home?

Elderly Female Funeral Home Owner: Uh-huh, what did you, would it have it be, uh, is it in the movie in regards to some funerals or something?

It's an exciting vampire movie, and there's a scene where Shaquille O'Neal is an evil vampire that must be stopped.

Mm-hmm.

So there would be a tremendous battle between Shaquille O'Neal and Brian Dennehy in your funeral home.

In my funeral home?

Yeah. *(pause)* Is that of interest to you?

(breathy exhalation) Yeah.

Okay, would you have any bodies there when we would shoot? They would not be harmed in any way, we have some very good pyrotechnic people, but I noticed that you do have the lifelike preservation, so I was hoping to have a few of those in the shot.

People who are already deceased… Well, I would have to get permission from, you know, I can't guarantee you, *(laughs)* I couldn't guarantee you that I'm going to have any bodies here. Because hey, you say it's going to be in the what? In the summer?

Right.

Uh-huh.

Summer's kind of a slow time for you?

As a rule it is. Most times, our business season is during the time of now, throughout to the early spring.

Oh, there's more people dying during the winter?

More people die when the sun goin' down in the fall of the year, and as the sun come up in the spring of the year, that's when you see it, it's seasonal. And then of course the other time is just, you know, accidental in the summer and drownings and you know, stuff like that, but it's not natural causes. Natural causes usually have nature taking its course during those months, from October through April, May. But sure, if I had some bodies here, then I'll secure getting permission from the family, because they would have to be satisfied with the fact that their loved ones are being shot and in a movie.

It will be a major motion picture, and maybe that would be one way for them to remember their loved ones, by being able to see them up on the big screen or by renting the video. I'm sure they would be excited about that.

Mm-hmm.

Plus, you would get to meet Shaquille O'Neal!

Well now are you serious or are you just talking?

Oh, no, I'm serious, well, you know, we're putting out feelers right now and trying to find locations for the shoot, just because we have some other shooting that we're going to be doing in Wisconsin.

Well, our facility is a quite nice facility, and it's in a nice neighborhood and all, uh, well then, you follow this up with a letter?

Sure, I could do that. Yeah, I could lay out exactly what kind of action sequences we're going to be doing, what sort of explosions. Again, we have done some scouting, and thought that your funeral home was very nice-looking, and had the scary mood that we were looking for. I can send you more of a concrete plan of what we would like to do.

Very good. And your name again?

My name is Mike Loew.

Mike Loew. And you're calling me from California?

That's right. Los Angeles. And I'm with Galactic Pictures.

Galactic Picture in California, mm-hmm.

 Well, I have your address, so I will get some materials together and get those out to you.

Very good.

 And I guess we'll just have to see if you have the bodies coming in at that time of the year, you know, maybe we could cross our fingers for some accidental drownings or something.

Yes, uh-huh.

 Sounds great! Thanks so much, you've been great.

You're more than welcome. Bye-bye.

The requested documents were hastily prepared at Galactic Studios and rushed to the funeral home...

NOTHING BUT NECK.

December 30, 1999

   Congratulations! You have been chosen to participate in *Shaqula,* the biggest blockbuster of the new millennium, starring Shaquille O'Neal as an insane vampire and Brian Dennehy as the crusty FBI agent who must stab him. I'm writing this to you from my desk in Los Angeles.

   O'Neal brings his tremendous rebounding and dunking skills to his performance as Shaquille O'Malley, a hot young basketball star who is bitten by a big hairy bat during a clutch free-throw attempt. He must battle his own vampirism as it threatens to derail his career, but his inner struggle is quickly dwarfed by the awesome explosions that soon surround him.

   With music by Aerosmith, Puff Daddy, Korn, and Shaquille himself, *Shaqula* is the timeless story of one man's struggle to stop eating human brains set to the rhythm of today's funky beat.

   Please contact me on my cel phone, which is (213) 432-... voice mailbox extension code dir... or at my office at Galactic Pictur... in my Humvee the number is 213-... I can also be contacted at my assi... my pager is built into my headset... via e-mail, which is loew@shaqula...

Cheers!

Mike Loew
Special Effects Coordinator

GALACTIC PICTURES   LOS ANG...

804. SHAQULA prepares to chomp.

McGRUFFIN: "Drop the head, Shaqula."

SHAQULA: "RAAAA"

805. SHAQ attack!

McGRUFFIN: "You're going down!"

806. McGRUFFIN strafes room, SHAQULA swiftly dodges and transforms into a vapor.

SPIRITUAL
DIALOGUE

Americans are once again nuzzling into God's bosom. Athletes give thanks and praise for every victory, politicians race each other up the church steps, and rousing hymns top the pop charts. Plus, recent studies show that those who attend church regularly on Sunday morning, avoiding strenuous Friday and Saturday night activities, live slightly longer lives. But where is the source of this raging Godmania? With only his faith to guide him, Mike Loew tracks down the biggest celebrity of all time through His/Her/Its agents on Earth.

JEHOVAH'S WITNESSES

 Hi, I'm calling because I was interested in joining your religion, but I was wondering if we could work out an arrangement.

Female Jehovah's Witness: What do you mean by that?

 I was thinking how I really respect the way the Jehovah's Witnesses go around to all the homes in the area to witness to the people out there, and since I own a pizza restaurant, I was wondering if your people could hand out my pizza coupons along with their Jehovah's Witness literature.

Okay, first of all, what is your name?

 Mike Loew.

Mike Loew? I'm Barb.

 Hi, Barb.

And people don't join Jehovah's Witnesses, Mike, what we do is conduct home Bible discussions with persons on various subjects, as to what the Bible teaches, like why do we grow old and die or why does God allow the wickedness, what is our hope for the future, what is God's Kingdom that we pray for? Uh, why do people die. So, we do Bible studies with them within a period of time so that they can get Bible answers to these questions, and then they can make a knowledgeable decision, based on knowledge if they want to become one of Jehovah's Witnesses. So that's our whole purpose, to teach the Bible and the hope that it holds out that God, very soon through His kingdom, which is a government, will make the Earth like a paradise, like how we started out with Adam and Eve, and how we can be a part of that if we so desire. And so that's our purpose, and so no one can join us, but you can become one of us, after a period of study, and we have—

 Okay, okay, do you think that I could start the period of study, and then the people in your organization could be passing out my pizza coupons right away?

No, like I said, our main purpose is to teach the Bible, so when we go door-to-door talking to people, we don't solicit funds, and we don't solicit any business. Our main purpose to be there is to teach the Bible, and so we keep it totally separate, it's not part of a business or anything.

Okay. Because I would be happy to become one of you if I could—

Well, what I can do is take your name and your address and have someone call on you to give you a brief demonstration of how we go about the study I was telling you about. And then you can decide, when they can come back or if they can come back.

Okay.

Okay, I'll write it down here, and your name is Mike Loew, you said?

Yeah.

Okay, there's a lot of pizza eaters in our acquaintance, so I don't think you're going to have to worry about pizza being sold, that's for sure.

Oh, okay, you think that I could—

I mean, people love pizza, so—*(laughs)*

Okay, do you have prayer meetings that I could turn into a big pizza party?

No, what I'll do is, when I take your address, when the person that calls, he will tell you a bit more about our meeting times and what goes on there. Okay? What is your address?

Address is *(provides address).*

Is that an apartment or a house?

Little bit of both.

Okay. And when would be a good time for them to call, Mike?

Oh, any time, really.

Okay, so you're there any day? What about tomorrow? If they came around 11:30 you would be there?

Yeah, that would work out.

Okay, well I'll arrange for somebody to stop in about that time.

I could have some of my pizza on hand, because it really is, I think, just awesome pizza.

Well, that would be up to you.

 And maybe the person would get excited about it and would want to help me spread the word about my pizza, too.

Well, okay, we'll see.

 Great.

Okay, so I'll have somebody there then.

CHURCH SUPPLY STORE

 Hi, this is Mike from Los Angeles. I'm a married Christian man, and I'm wondering if your store stocks any Christian pornography.

Male Church Supplier: Say again.

 I'm looking for pornography featuring married Christian couples. My wife and I were hoping to enjoy some materials that were more Christ-oriented.

Sorry, I have no idea what you're talking about.

 Well, standard pornography doesn't really follow Christian principles, and I was hoping to find videos or magazines with married, loving couples—

Never seen it, never heard of it.

 Do you know of any Web sites that I could visit?

No idea. I would check Faithful Flock Bookstore, let me give you their number. *(provides number)* Good luck. Bye-bye.

FAITHFUL FLOCK BOOKSTORE

 Hi, I was just referred to you from the Church Supply Store.

Female Bookstore Employee: Oh, great!

 Anyway, I'm looking for some Christian pornography. Does your store stock any?

No…

 I'm a married man, and my wife and I were hoping to find some videos or magazines that would have married Christian couples making love in a Christian setting.

No, but I think you better get another book, why don't you come in here and I'll show you a few, okay, that would help you out a whole lot more.

 What sort of books?

Books on growing in your marriage, and, I have a whole bunch of things that would really be helpful to you. Okay?

 Is there any pornography in your books?

I don't think you need that. I think you need a couple of other things. Okay? Why don't you come in?

 Could you tell me more about your books and what I might find in there, ma'am?

I can see about five of them from right here. They're all on relationships, and building strong relationships, and if you are hoping to gain in your physical area, you will gain in that as well, but marriage is a full, composite thing, so in order to grow in one you have to grow in all the others as well.

 I am very interested in my physical area.

So I would recommend you coming in and asking for Paul, he's the store manager here. Thank you.

ADULT BOOKSTORE

 Hi, I'm a married man and my wife and I are Christians, so I'm wondering if your store stocks any Christian pornography.

Male Adult Bookstore Employee: No, we don't.

 Okay, I'm looking for models who are married, couples who are married...

Yeah, there's a lot of like, uh, so you're looking for porn where the couples are actually married in it?

 That would work.

Yeah, there's a couple of Andrew Blake flicks that are like that, and some Candita Royale.

 Are those people Christians?

I don't know if they're Christian.

 Any other stuff that might have a Christian feel, or have a church theme to it...

Honestly, probably not.

 What about magazines? Do you have any Christian porn magazines?

No, we don't.

 Well, what sort of porn would you recommend? Because my wife and I are Christian, but we like to enjoy the pornography together, so do you have any stuff there that would fit our lifestyle?

Honestly, the only thing that I can tell you is that we do have couple-oriented porn. As far as the whole religion aspect goes, I don't really know what to tell you, but there is couple-oriented porn out there. All right? Have a good one.

 Okay, I guess I'll come in and check out that porn with the couples in it. God bless you.

Yup.

INDIAN CASINO

 Hi, I'd like to have a solemn religious ceremony in front of your building.

Female Receptionist: Hold on one moment, I'm going to transfer you to our security department.

(on hold)

Security Woman: Security, can I help you?

 Hi, my name is Mike and I'm calling because I enjoy coming to your casino and gambling there with my friends, and a few of those friends and I have worked out a religious system where we give prayers and offerings to the Sacred Bingo Goddess before we go in to gamble. I was wondering if it would be okay to have a little prayer circle in front of the building before we went in this weekend, and burn some sage and do some dancing for our religious ceremony.

Oh, wow, what day were you going to plan on doing that?

 We were hoping to come up tomorrow.

Okay, what time about?

 Probably around noon, when the Bingo Goddess is strongest.

Okay, can I put you on hold for a minute, and find out who exactly you need to speak to for doing that? Okay, hold on.

(on hold)

Security Man: Security Director speaking, can I help you?

 Hi, my name is Mike, and I'm calling because a few of my friends and I have worked out a religious system where we give prayers and offerings to the Sacred Bingo Goddess before we go in to gamble.

What was your name again, Mike—

 Mike Loew, yes. We were wondering if we could do a little prayer circle and maybe some dancing and burn some sacred herbs in front of the building right before we go in. We just thought it would be more efficacious to do the ceremony right before we went in to gamble.

You want to do that in front of the Bingo Hall?

 Yeah, in front would be harmonious, but if you had to put us out in the back, I guess that would be okay.

And how many people?

 We have ten people. Sort of a small group of believers.

Well, you know, this is not a religious environment. I mean, everyone has their religion and everything like that. I try to have respect for everybody's beliefs and everything. Isn't there some way that you guys could do this at your own home or something like that?

 Yeah, that's what we have been doing, but then we have to drive an hour-and-a-half up there, and it seems like the prayers lose their power as time goes by. We thought that if we could do them right before we went in, they would work better.

You know, I'm kind of a strong believer in prayer, you know, and I believe that if you really believe in what you're doing, then you could be all the way across the whole United States and if you really believe that, well then, you pray for somebody over there, or whatever, then it's going to be that way.

 I think I follow you.

You've gotta have faith in your prayers.

 Well, you know how it is when you sit down at the bingo table, you just really want to feel that you're lucky, you want to feel like you've got someone pulling for you, and we really do get that nice feeling from our prayers.

Who are you guys going to pray to now?

 The Sacred Bingo Goddess.

Bingo Goddess, okay.

So we could be well away from the building, or out in the back, I guess that would be okay.

Well, what do you guys use? You know, we have, Native Americans have religious things that we use.

We've taken some of those elements, some bits and pieces, so we burn some sage, and we do have a powwow drum.

Powwow?

You know, the flat drum that sits on the ground and three guys sit around it and hit it.

Okay, what else you gotta do? You sing?

Yeah, we do some singing, you know, like "O Bingo Goddess, sacred and powerful, you make the little round ball pop up just right."

How long does this take?

About three hours.

Do you have a phone number where I could call you?

Sure, it's *(provides number)*.

Okay, I'm going to have to talk to my supervisor about that, the general manager, and get a confirmation. Otherwise, like I was saying, they don't usually have too many religious activities here on the premises, because it is a gambling casino. Like you say, if you could do it at your home, and believe in your prayers, and have faith that that's going to be that way, then that's going to be that way. But I'll get back to you. You're going to be there?

Yeah, sure, I'm just sewing up our costumes here.

I'll see what I can find out right away.

ISLAMIC CENTER

Hi, my name is Mike Loew, and I'm with FunRaisers, a local fund raising company. We're putting together a big event with a number of religious organizations in town, and I was wondering if your center would be interested in participating!

Islamic Male: Fund raising for what?

 We're raising funds for various churches and synagogues in the area with a big bikini car wash. All money raised from the bikini car wash, besides the operating costs, will go to the religious organizations involved. Would your center be interested in taking part in the bikini car wash?

No, thank you.

 Oh, you're not interested?

No, thanks.

 Any reason why? There's all sorts of exciting things that are going to be happening that day, we have a number of models from a top modeling agency—

Just for religious reasons. We are not supposed to participate in stuff like that.

 Oh, you're not supposed to participate in car washes?

No, bikini car washes.

 There's a problem with the bikinis?

I believe so.

 Okay. Anything we can fix? The models are very professional, and they're also very nice ladies. I'm sure they would try hard to not make you feel uncomfortable.

I know that, thank you very much for the offer anyways, but it is not right.

 Well, I can respect your decision, but you sure are missing out here, buddy.

Hello, God? It's me, Michael. Call me back sometime.

VIDEO GAME COMPANY

 Hi, my name's Mike Loew, I'm calling because my son has been playing your video game, *Kazok 2: Hordes of Evil* quite a bit lately, and he's really out of control. He's reenacting scenes from the video game all the time.

Female Representative: How old is he?

 He's eight.

Okay, do you realize that it's a mature-rated game and it's for 17-plus?

 Oh, geez, I didn't really catch that.

Yeah, it's listed on the front package of the game. All games are rated by the ESRB, so you have to make sure to check that before purchasing it. It's just like how movies are.

 I guess the damage is already done to his little brain, though, because I was unaware of what the symbols mean on the ratings. Do you have any ideas on how to deal with this? He's running around in a loincloth, he's asking me where I'm hiding the plasma cannon in the house—

If you want to exchange it for a different game, we can do that. He has *Kazok 2* for the N64?

 Yeah.

Let me see what we have in stock that is age-appropriate for him, okay? Hold on one moment.

(on hold)

Hi, sir? We have *Crazy Racers*, which is a car-racing game, and it's rated "E" for Everyone, if you want to exchange it for that, or, does he like sports? We have *Baseball 2000* or *Football 2000*.

 Maybe the football would be a good nonviolent game. I don't know if it's appropriate for an eight-year-old to be driving around like a crazy person.

Well, *Crazy Racers* is a remote-control car game, so that's what it is,

it's not really—

He's not driving around killing pedestrians?

No, no.

That sounds good, but do you have any tips on how I could get this out of his system? Yesterday I caught Tyler trying to ride around on our dog, and he was calling the dog his "warbeast"—

No, I don't know about that, you'd have to speak to someone about that.

Well, that's what I'm doing, right? You've never had any complaints about the content of your games before?

No, no. Because most people, they check the ratings on the games.

I guess I'm special. So these ratings are on—

Are on every single game. All games are rated by the ESRB. But I'm not really sure, if you're having problems with him, you'd have to speak to someone else, a counselor or something, maybe. But if you wanted to exchange it for that game, that's fine. What you have to do is send the game into us by UPS or certified mail, or FedEx, just make sure that you send it in a traceable way. And do you have our address?

Yeah, I have the manual for the game here. Let's see, enemies, weapons, multiplayer death match, blood color options, rotting corpses, okay, there's your address.

So you said you wanted to exchange that for *Football 2000* for the N64?

Let's do that.

Maybe then once he starts playing that, he'll be more focused on that.

That would be great. I'm tired of him zooming in on my head with his Nerf gun.

Or *Baseball 2000*, that's a lot of fun. I don't know if he enjoys baseball at all.

Does anybody?

Really, it's a fun game.

 So I just have to send this game back to you—

Yes. Just put "Attention: Consumer Service" on it, please, and just write that you'd like to exchange it for *Football 2000*.

 Okay, do you have some other games that are similar to *Kazok 2: Hordes of Evil* that I should keep my eye out for?

Just always make sure that you look at the packaging, and just look at the ratings. Every single video game, no matter which company it's by, you have to check the packaging and see who it's rated for.

 Oh, "M" stands for Mature, I get it. But "M" could be anything, I mean, it could stand for Mild or Mellow or Melodic or Matronly or—

It's just like if you were going to go the store and purchase a movie, and it's rated "R" or "PG" or whatever it's rated, you just have to check video games, too. All games are rated by the ESRB. If you ever have any questions about games, and about how they're rated, that's who you'd contact.

 So M is for Mature, and that's for evil-dinosaur-killing games for mature people, okay.

Yes, 17-plus. You'd want to purchase a game that's "E" for Everyone. Okay? Thank you.

FILLING THE
RANKS

In this volatile world of post-Cold War geopolitics, a huge and well-trained military is our best weapon in the fight for world peace. Posing as a variety of applicants, Mike Loew tests the judgment of our military recruiters, who bear the awesome responsibility of choosing America's defenders.

MISSION 1: THE U.S. NAVY

 Hi, this is Mike and I'm calling from Los Angeles because I want to join the Navy.

Male Naval Recruiter: Okay.

 Yeah, um, that's what I want to do.

Let me ask you a few questions. Are you a high school graduate?

 I'm going to finish this May.

So you're a senior in school right now.

 Yep.

Do you have any police involvement?

 Oh, no.

Any minor traffic violations?

 No, my parents don't let me drive the car.

That helps. Do you have anything medically wrong with you? Asthma, any allergies?

 No.

Ever been hospitalized for anything? Ever seen, um, what do you call it, a psychiatrist?

 Well, I was having a lot of problems in school with girls and stuff, so I saw a therapist once. Actually, I'm calling because I thought being in the Navy, with the uniform and everything, maybe I could meet some girls. Is that what happens in the Navy?

(chuckles) More than likely, yeah.

 Wow! Have you been around the world and stuff?

A little bit.

 Do girls really dig guys in the Navy?

It depends. It's more the uniform than anything else.

That's what I was thinking!

So when do you think you could come in here? What's your name?

Mike Loew.

When could you come in, Mike? We'd like to talk to you, tell you what's available. You won't be able to go to boot camp until you get your diploma, but you can be on the delayed entry program, and you can sign up ahead of time.

Are there any girls in boot camp?

Oh, yeah.

Wow, is it like a party, or do guys have to stay in their own rooms and stuff?

I'm not sure how they do it—I think it's separate companies, where the men and the women are separated, and you go from there. But there's no problem, especially after boot camp.

Really? Is it just a golden land of opportunity?

It's what you make of it.

When you were out there, were there a lot of girls and stuff?

You could say that. I was down in San Diego when I was in boot camp, and there was definitely the opportunity. I had a girlfriend at the time, so I didn't—

I wish I had a girlfriend.

(*uncomfortable pause*) Tell you what, can you come in after school on Friday?

Sure!

Do you know where our office is located, Mike?

Yeah, my parents can drive me there. Um, when I come in, could you tell me, like, where the best bases to meet girls are?

Well, you know what, wherever you're stationed at, there's not going to be a problem. If you get on a ship and head overseas, there won't be a problem. If that's what you want to do, there is no problem.

 Is it really all in the uniform?

Pretty much so.

 Wow, can you give me an example of how it goes? Like, do you pull into port, and go to a bar...

I tell you what, we can explain that even more when you come in. We can even show you pictures.

 PICTURES?!?

Of the opportunities that are available. We can explain it a lot better in person than over the phone.

 Pictures of girls, or pictures of places to meet girls, or pictures of—

Kind of both. We don't have any of the nude shots or anything like that, but, well... you'll see.

 Wow, I can't wait! Can you give me an idea so I can think about it and stuff?

Um, I really can't.

 Are they top secret?

No...

 Does the Navy, like, keep secret files on where all the girls are?

No, you've got to come in, we'll sit and talk, and if that's what you want to do, there wouldn't be a problem. You could go to any bar, and if you wanted to pick up a chick, you probably could. It's just a matter of saying the right thing.

 Could you teach me lines to say and stuff, Sergeant?

Any line would work, sometimes. Just come in here after school tomorrow, around four, and we'll discuss it, and we'll go from there.

And I can look at the photos and everything?

We'll show you, Mike.

 Awesome! I'll see you then.

MISSION 2: THE U.S. ARMY

 Hi, I'm calling from Los Angeles because I'm interested in joining the Army.

Male Army Recruiter: Okay.

 I do have some questions. I'm a religious person, and I'm wondering if there would be any problems with my religion.

What religion are you?

 I'm a Buddhist. The problem is that Buddhism really values the sanctity of human life, and I can't take a life. But I'd still really love to be in the Army.

So are you a conscientious objector?

 Oh no, not at all. I'd love to be in the Army—I've loved the commercials I've seen. They're very exciting. It's just that I couldn't kill anyone.

Well, I'll tell you what, partner. There's a lot of jobs in the Army where probably a meteor would fall on you before you'd have to kill somebody. But a recruiter would be lying to you if he said that there wasn't a chance that you might have to do that. And that goes for any job in any of the armed services, because we're the Armed Forces of the United States. The possibility is there. It doesn't matter if you're a cook, a dentist, a truck driver, a chaplain's assistant—

 Chaplains' assistants have to kill people?

Well, the chaplain's assistant still has to shoot and qualify with an M16 rifle and a .45-caliber pistol. The possibility could arise that the enemy could attack. Would you protect your family?

Hmm...

If somebody walked into your house right now and was going to kill your parents.

 Well, there's always reincarnation.

I can put it to you like this. If you were face to face in an alley right now, in a city in the United States, and that person was going to kill you, and you knew that... Let's say you wandered into the wrong street. It happens every day in America. Would you defend your life?

 That's a good question. There is the whole turning the other cheek thing.

Well, I agree with turning the other cheek, you know, I'm a civilized person myself. I'm a Christian, but there's... I mean, once you're dead, you're dead.

 We can always hope to come back as a higher life form.

No, I agree with you...

 So could I be a chaplain's assistant?

Hey, you pick your own job in the Army. Absolutely. But you're still going to have to qualify with a weapon. You're still going to be trained to defend yourself.

 Could there maybe be a different way to deal with the enemy? Could I try to spread a message of peace?

(chuckles) You know, you could spend twenty years in the Army and never go to war. It's happened. But I can't say that it won't happen. World War Three could start up two years from now and you might get drafted. They could reinstate the draft—you never know. But you know, we promote peace right now. We're on peacekeeping operations, other than war, throughout the world. We've got 32,000 soldiers right now promoting peace in Bosnia. But we're promoting peace through the presence of a powerful military. Just by you wearing an American uniform, you're promoting peace.

 Yes, I am really interested in spreading peace, and the Army seems like a great place to do it.

Are you a high school graduate?

Yeah, I graduated a few years ago.

So what are you doing now?

Just working. On the weekends I like to meditate and burn incense. But I've gotten tired of my job, and I thought the Army might be a good place to really concentrate on Buddhism.

Hold on a sec. Yeah, okay... You know, Buddhism is recognized as a religion in the Army. So would you be interested in sitting down and talking to a recruiter?

That sounds very positive.

Hey, I'm going to put you on the phone with a high-speed young lady who would be more than happy to help you out. What's your name?

Mike Loew.

Okay, Mike, hold on.

Female Army Recruiter: Mike? Could you tell me a little about yourself?

Well, I've gotten tired of my job, and I thought the Army would be a good place to go. My one problem is that I am a practicing Buddhist and cannot take life of any sort. I mean, I have to watch where I step so I don't kill any ants—I don't know how fast I could go through those obstacle courses.

Well, when would you like to sit down and talk?

Oh, whenever—time has little meaning for me—but do you think my concerns will be a problem?

The running shouldn't be a problem, hurting or killing anything. The other thing is, I've been in the Army for eight years, and I've never had to kill anybody. And I spent six months in Saudi Arabia.

How was that?

It was scary.

Have you ever practiced transcendental meditation?

No, I haven't.

 It's great, it really drives away scary feelings. I was thinking about getting into the Army and trying to get other soldiers into meditation and prayer—basically Buddhist contemplations on the sanctity of life.

Well, yeah.

 Do you think I could do some of that in boot camp?

Sure. Um, when would you like to talk?

 Tomorrow?

What time is good for you?

 About four o'clock?

Okay. Could I get your full name?

 It's Michael Andrew Loew, although I'm known at the temple as Golden Feather of Harmony.

Are you a graduate?

 Yes.

Where did you graduate from?

 Appleton East High School. I was a Buddhist at that time too. I started up a group to stop the football program because I thought it was too violent. I thought that the players should just talk about their differences on the field.

All right. Where were you born?

 Milwaukee, Wisconsin.

Can I get your date of birth?

 It's March 14, 1973.

How is your health? Um, do you have asthma, how are your knees, stuff like that.

Well, I'm really flexible because I do a lot of yoga. And I'm also a vegan, I don't eat any foods of animal origin, so that keeps me healthy.

Could I get your height and weight?

I'm 6'7", 290 pounds.

Are you married?

No, I'm a celibate monk.

So you don't have any children?

No, I'm more of a child myself, of my spiritual leader, the Dalai Lama.

All right. And do you have any law violations that I should be aware of?

I did get into a little trouble. I went to the large animal holding facility on campus, because I thought it was unjust that they were holding the cows there. I tried to set them free, so I got into some trouble, but it was just a misdemeanor. Cows are very sacred in my religion.

Okay. Do you have any other questions for me?

Do you think that me setting the cows free is going to be a problem?

Well, if it's just a misdemeanor, it shouldn't affect anything.

Okay. So can you assure me that I will find an outlet for peace in the Army? The man was telling me that the Army is a peacekeeping organization, and that's what I want to do.

That's what we've been trying to do for a long time. Our missions to Somalia and Saudi Arabia were to help people out.

How about bombing Serbia? Was that a peaceful mission?

Yes, it was.

Boy, if I can keep peace in the Army, that's the place for me.

Great. Well, I will see you tomorrow at four. You know where we are?

Yes, I have the address. Um, four o'clock falls right around my ritual prayer time. Would it be okay if I brought in some of my little bells and showed you a few of the prayers I do?

Well, I'm not too sure about doing that in here, Mike. Did you want to make it for a later time?

No, I guess I can just do some speed-meditation before I come in.

All right, if you don't have any other questions, I'll see you tomorrow around four.

Great. I wish you a very serene day.

Thank you very much, Mike. You have a good day, too.

Peace.

MISSION 3: THE U.S. MARINES

Hi, I'm calling because I've been thinking about joining the Marines.

Male Marine Recruiter: Okay. Let me go back to my desk. What's your name?

Mike Loew. Yeah, I was calling because I've seen the ads and everything, and I really love the game of chess. The commercial really grabbed me.

Okay.

Are there a lot of opportunities in the Marine Corps for chess clubs, chess tournaments, that kind of thing?

Yeah, I never got into that stuff, but I imagine there would be Special Services or something.

Is there a special Chess Force battalion?

Not really special chess clubs or anything, but there's always military organizations that you could get into later on.

Later on?

When you're in.

Great. And of course, the swords are great too. Does every Marine get a sword like that?

I really don't know.

Do you have a sword?

No. Where are you calling from, Mike?

Los Angeles.

Do you know anyone from your school who enlisted in the Marine Corps?

Not really, I was too busy with the chess club.

What is your interest with the Marine Corps?

You know, the commercial really did it for me. I love the medieval costumes and the evil wizard throwing the fireball. I love the knight on horseback. I think it sounds like a really exciting organization, to have chess games enacted full-scale with costumed human pieces. It's a real innovation for chess that I would love to be a part of.

We really don't do that. That's pretty much the advertising, to draw the attention.

Oh, that's disappointing. So you don't do any live-action medieval chess games at all?

No, nothing like you see on TV. Tell you what, let me get your address so I can send you some information.

Okay. (*provides address*) Could you at least send me a cool poster of that chess battle?

If I can find anything, I'll see what I can do.

Have you seen that commercial?

That one's old, yeah, but I've seen it.

Do you know if there are going to be more awesome chess commercials?

I don't know. Well, all right, man, you have a good one.

Okay, 'bye.

MISSION 4: THE U.S. AIR FORCE

Hello, this is Mike from Los Angeles! I'm interested in joining the Air Force.

Male Air Force Recruiter: Okay. Let me get some information from you. What is your name?

Mike Loew.

Are you a high school grad?

I am.

What year?

Ninety-one. You know, I want to join because I recently got out of a relationship. Things are okay now between us, but I thought I should move on and meet some other men.

Okay, let me ask you some qualifying questions here. How tall are you?

I'm 5'2".

Weight?

One hundred fifteen pounds. I'm sure I would fit quite nicely in the cockpit, and I have perfect 20/20 vision. I really do love your planes. Of course, the uniforms are beautiful too.

Mmm-hmm.

I was wondering about the social activities in the Air Force. Are there dance nights? I am just crazy about Ricky Martin, so I was thinking about starting a fan club with the other men.

I don't know about that. Let me ask some more questions here. Any law violations?

 Well, I was involved in an ACT-UP demonstration—

In what?

 ACT-UP, it's an AIDS activist group, the AIDS Coalition to Unleash Power. We demonstrated in front of the governor's office, there was a sit-in, then some commotion, and I got some little disturbing-the-peace charge.

Disturbing the peace?

 Yeah, the cops showed up, and me and Rick and Steve and Bruce all had to spend the night in jail. But we were out the next day, and I was able to show up for my afternoon shift at the salon.

What other violations?

 Let me think… There was this one time when some guy on the street got in my face, when I was with my friend—

Let me make this easier for you. Just tell me the charges, not the stories.

 Right, a man came up and he didn't like that we were holding hands, and—

Hold it. Let's start over. Tell me the charge you were charged with, no story.

 Oh, it was a fighting charge. We were outside of a bar, and this guy didn't like the looks of Rick and me, and things just got out of hand.

(*chuckles*) I'd say they would. Give me another law violation.

 I'd say that's about it. Sometimes my friends charge me with violating the laws of good taste with the outfits I wear when we go dancing, but let's not even go there!

Okay, let's talk about drug usage.

 Not much, maybe some ecstacy at a rave once in a while.

Some what?

Ecstacy, it makes you all loose and happy. It's a nice little party favor. Nothing heavy-duty.

Ec-sta-cy. What other drugs?

 Oh, maybe a little Chardonnay at dinner, that's all.

Have you ever been hospitalized?

 Oh, after that fight I had a few stitches put in, but I've found that a little rouge hides the scar quite well.

Give me a moment here. Looking up a few things for you.

 Yes, that relationship ending with Rick really makes me want to get out of town. I haven't asked yet, but is there any problem with my sexual orientation?

Well, to tell you the truth, I'm getting ready to make you ineligible here for the Air Force based on questionable moral character. Maybe gender identity disorder, something like that. And you've got some things here I'm not used to dealing with. I don't think you're going to be eligible based on the things you're telling me here.

 I thought that I could bring some diversity to the Air Force.

Yeah, I'm sure. It would be quite diverse.

 Do you think I would have trouble fitting in with the other men?

Well, I don't think you're eligible.

 Because I'm gay?

Now, I didn't ask you that, did I?

 No.

Okay, I'm saying that you're ineligible due to what I would call questionable moral character, gender identity or other things.

 I always have been a little confused about my gender...

Yeah. Sure.

But I wouldn't call that a disorder. There's a little bit of woman in every man and a little bit of man in every woman.

Well, I'm glad that you can assess that for yourself.

 Do you ever get in touch with your feminine side?

I'll tell you what, at this time it looks like you're ineligible for the Air Force. I appreciate your call, and I'm going to end this conversation now.

 Can I get back to you at any point, could things change, or is the door slamming in my face here?

I can't see where things would change.

 Maybe if... Who's in charge of the Air Force? The Chief Pilot Officer?

Yeah, right.

 What if he turned out to be gay? If a gay man was in charge, maybe things could change and I could be in the Air Force.

There's always room for changes. Well, I've got some other work to take care of, and I appreciate your call, and at this time you are ineligible for the Air Force. Okay?

 Okay, thanks, sweetie.

After a long, courageous struggle to win acceptance for gays in the military, Mike Loew is now flamboyantly vaporizing America's enemies with laser-guided bombs.

HOSPITAL

 Hi, my name is Mike Loew, and I'm hoping to make an appointment. I want to give my nipples to your organ donor program.

Female Receptionist: Okay... Can you hold a second?

(on hold)

Okay, hello? I can give you the number. This is called Organ Procurement. The number is *(provides number).* And I can connect you.

 Oh, great. Thank you.

(on hold)

Different Female Receptionist: Good morning, Organ Procurement.

 Hi, I'm calling because I want to donate my nipples to your program. Just because I'm not really using them, and I thought that they could really help someone out.

Okay, this office that you have called works with donors that have passed away, so I can transfer you to our Transplant Office, and they work with living donors. Okay? Hold on.

(on hold)

Transplant Office: Transplant Office, this is Valerie.

 Hi, I'm calling because I'm hoping to donate my nipples to the organ donor program there. Just because I'm not really using them. *(total silence from Valerie)* **And I was just transferred to you because you do transplants from living people.** *(more silence)* **And I'm a living person.**

And you want to donate what?

 My nipples. Both of them.

Just a moment.

(on hold)

I'm sorry, we don't do that.

 Oh, but I was thinking that women who have undergone a mastectomy could use them, or perhaps people who have suffered a serious nipple injury. I don't really use them, so they're all yours if you want 'em.

Well, I've never heard of anybody doing that, and we deal with mostly liver, pancreas, and kidneys up in this office. Now the only other place that I can think of—did you try the Breast Clinic?

 No, I didn't.

Let me transfer you down there, but really, honestly, I've never, ever heard of anybody doing anything like that, ever. But let me switch you down to the Breast Clinic.

(on hold)

Breast Clinic: Good morning, Breast Clinic, this is Caroline, may I help you?

 Hi, I was just transferred to you. I'm hoping to donate my nipples to the organ donor program at your hospital. Just because I don't need them for anything, and perhaps a woman who had to go through a mastectomy could use them.

Well, let's see, I am not sure how that would work. Uh…

 They seem like a vestigial, functionless, evolutionary mistake on me, so I just thought it would be nice to share.

Well, I don't know, we could almost even refer you to Organ Procurement, as a possibility.

 Yeah, I spoke with Organ Procurement for the dead people and the living people, and then they transferred me to you, so it looks like the Breast Clinic is the end of the line.

Okay, this almost seems like a plastics issue, being that after a woman has had a mastectomy, there is breast reconstruction. So that might be a possibility.

 Or athletes who get a bad nipple injury.

Right. Okay, I hate to keep transferring you, but a person that might be able to address this type of offer would be Dr. Schmidt's secretary Tammy. So if you'll hold, I'll transfer you to Tammy. Thank you so much.

(on hold)

Dr. Schmidt's Office: Good morning, Dr. Schmidt's office, this is Tammy.

 Hi, Tammy, I was just transferred to you from the Breast Clinic.

Yes!

 I was wondering if I could donate my nipples to your hospital? Just because I'm not really using them, and I thought that there must be all sorts of people who would enjoy them more than me.

Okay, that I don't know, I think typically they reconstruct them, but let me check on that, okay? Thank you.

(on hold)

Sir, I did confirm that they do reconstruct them from the person's own tissue. Okay?

 So there's no use for mine?

There's not, no. But thank you.

 There's nothing wrong with them. They're perfectly fine nipples.

I'm sorry, but we cannot use them at this time.

 If you need to let technology catch up with my idea, you could put my nipples in a cryogenic deep-freeze, then thaw them out when you're ready to use them. That wouldn't bother me.

Again, thank you for thinking of us, sir. Have a nice day.

IT'S A
CRIME

Violent crime rates are dropping, but recent studies show that American children still see an average of 5,000 murders by the time they turn eighteen. Television also contains many scenes of violence. Crime surrounds us, yet its root causes, socioeconomic context, and most successful strategies are not easily understood. With a microphone firmly taped to his chest, Mike Loew buttons up and goes undercover for the answers.

CARPET CLEANER

 Hi, I was wondering if you could get blood out of a carpet.

Carpet Cleaning Man: Yes, how much was spilled?

 Boy, there's a fair amount. It's a stain about five feet across.

Okay, five feet across could be very little blood or it could be a lot of blood. Uh, can you tell me what happened? It will make it a little easier for me to figure out what we're doing.

 Geez, it all happened so quickly. Basically, someone got stabbed.

Nobody bled to death.

 No, not exactly. Other things were involved.

Okay, so someone got stabbed, they have a fair amount of blood on the floor. The question that I have is—I'm just trying to figure this out—is whether or not the blood has gone into the backing or is still sitting up in the yarn.

 I think I definitely soaked it all the way to the backing.

Okay, what room is this?

 Most of it is in the living room. Some blood on the walls, too.

Okay. If we find that it's in the backing, then we should be cleaning it both from the back and the front. Yes, even if it went all the way down to the backing, we are able to get it out.

 Cool. Because some of my blood is on the floor, too, which is bad.

Blood never comes out, though, unless it's a few drops, in one pass. You have to come back at least once, usually three times, because blood dilutes. When you go after it with the right chemical, it's going to dilute. As soon as it dilutes, you're pulling out of there about 5 percent blood, 95 percent water. When that dries, you're still going to see a little bit of that stain. It doesn't matter how many times you rinse—we could stay there and rinse till we're dead—the next day, we're still going to see some of that stain. It has to dry, then has to be dissolved again, and then either the second or the third time that we go after it, it is totally gone.

Okay, how quickly could you do a procedure like that?

Well, of course, if it wasn't for the holiday, I'd say either tonight or tomorrow. Are you going to have company over at your house for Thanksgiving?

Actually, I don't live here, so I need to have this done as soon as possible. I do have another question—

Sure.

Can you get small hairs out of carpets? Can you do some heavy vacuuming in here?

Yeah, you would want to do a heavy vacuuming—is this dog hair we're talking about?

No, human hair, my hair. I don't want to leave any stray hairs behind.

Okay, you'd want to do a vacuuming. Then, if you're concerned about that area, we would use what's called a PowerGlide, which extracts but does it in a rotary manner. And as it's spinning, it tends to curl the hair up and make it into little hairballs. So we can get 99 percent of that out. But frankly, you still need to vacuum the next day. Because some of those hairs are very, very tiny, and will not come through the extractor. So after it dries, I tell people to make sure that they vacuum.

Thanks for the tip. I will definitely do that.

What is your name?

It's Mike... Bradshaw. One more question—could you do a process to get carpet fibers off of my body and my clothing? I don't want any fibers on me or in my car from this house, so do you have a cleaning process like that?

Sure. Yes, we can do that. What's your phone number?

It's (provides number).

And where are you located?

Yeah, I guess you need to know that. Let's see, where am I—okay, here we go, here's a piece of mail. I'm at *(provides address)*.

And the number where you're at is something we can call you back at in about an hour?

 Yeah, I guess I can stick around. I need to leave town relatively quickly, though.

Well, I'll have my wife call you for scheduling as soon as possible.

 Okay, great. Finally, out of curiousity, after you do your cleaning and extract all this DNA evidence, how do you dispose of the waste?

That gets sanitized and goes into a sanitary sewer.

 So it's a pretty discreet dumping?

Yes.

 It just disappears and you never see it again?

Correct. Right down the drain.

 Okay, sounds great. I'll just hold tight here and wait for your call.

All right, thank you, Mr. Bradshaw.

CRIME STOPPERS

 Hi, I wanted to report a crime of vandalism.

Male Crime Stopper: Is this something that just occurred?

 Well, I'm not sure when it exactly occurred, but I just saw the damage, and wanted to report that to you.

Let me have you talk to our dispatcher.

Male Dispatcher: Dispatch.

 Hi, I need to report a crime of vandalism.

Okay, and where did this occur?

It's in the Taco Bell at 5324 Hollywood Boulevard.

And what kind of vandalism?

 Well, I was in the men's restroom there with my eight-year-old son, and we were just washing our hands at the sink when I noticed that the bathroom hand dryer had been vandalized. Certain letters had been scratched off so that instead of "Push Button" it said "Push Butt," and instead of "Rub Hands Gently Under Warm Air" it said "Rub Hands Gently Under Arm"—

(disgusted at the crime) Ah, sheeesh. Kids with too much time on their hands. Are you a customer there, or an employee?

 I was a customer there. Possibly for the last time.

Okay, are you still at the Taco Bell?

 No, I'm giving you a call from my home. My son is running around here now pushing his butt and rubbing his hands in his armpits, and that is not a welcome development.

Okay, and what is your last name?

 Loew.

And first name?

 First name Mike. *(aside)* Tyler, stop rubbing!

And what's the address at home?

 My address is *(provides address)*.

That's Los Angeles?

 Yeah.

And what's the phone number there?

 Phone number is *(provides number)*.

Okay, we'll have a squad check on it.

Is there anything else that can be done about this?

Did you talk to the manager? We take the report on the vandalism, but he would be the one who would have to correct it. The only sure way to get something done is talk to Taco Bell, see if they wanted to pursue anything on it, and I am sure that they would want to act on this. But I definitely have the information.

 Great. Oh, one more thing is that they replaced "Reduces paper towel litter" with "Reduces ape litter." Now that is an image that does not promote healthy thoughts.

I agree, sir. I'm sorry you had to experience that.

 So is my son.

We're on our way over there.

 Thank you, Officer.

GATED COMMUNITY

 Hi, my name's Mike, and I'm new to the Los Angeles area. I'm interested in your gated community, but I'm curious about security issues, because I had a few problems getting into a gated community once before. Could I ask you a few questions about security?

Female Director: Certainly.

 So is the community in fact gated?

Yes, it is. We have three gates—are you looking at private homes or condominiums?

 Doesn't matter. Whatever's easiest.

Okay, the highway divides it, so there's one on the lake side that has a gate going into the community, and on the other side, there is a gate on the end of the private homes and on the end of the condominiums.

And how do the gates work?

You have a clicker in your car, that you push to open it, and when you go out they open automatically. During construction time, though, we do keep our gates open Monday through Friday, till 5:00.

 Excellent, I will make a note of that...

There's a lot of construction going on.

 Do you have walls around the whole community?

No, we do not. I think there's one other condominium project that has gates, but there's only the two gated communities in the immediate area. There's homes that abut the condominiums on the one side, it is not walled. Also, it's on a golf course—have you ever been out here?

 No, I haven't cased it out yet.

Okay, so we're sitting on a golf course, but there are not walls that go all the way around.

 Do you have any hidden security features like cameras or infrared beams on the grounds?

No, we do not. When you pull up—say you have a guest coming—and they were to pull up and that guest does not know how to get in the gate, they would page through and find your last name, and that would be a separate code. They would call up to your house, you would have to answer that—it can't be a wireless, it has to be a hard phone—and then you would hear them, and if you wanted them you would push "seven." Other than that, there are some other codes. Say you needed something and it was your mother that was coming in, and you weren't going to be home, and she didn't have a little clicker to come in. You could give her a code, your own private code, and she would have to push "enter" first, and then the four-digit code.

 Four digits, okay, not bad. Is there a sample code you could give me, or a universal code that people use for mother emergencies?

Uh, we try not to. Because then it just opens it all the way up. We do give the realtors on our team a code with which they can come in. And our newspapers are delivered in the morning, or at night or whenever, and they come early in the morning, so they have to be here within a specified amount of time, to get in to deliver the papers, or they can't get in on their code. So yes, it is the best system we can have in this area.

 So do you have any security guards or watch dogs on the premises?

No, on Halloween we always pull somebody in, just because the golf course is such a vast area, and that's the only time. As far as robberies and that, we've had none that I know of.

 That could always change.

Well, it's a new community, I think the first home was moved into in '95, and the first condo probably '95 or '96. So, it is a new community, you know, our offices are right here on the premises, and literally the developer of the whole golf course and the whole thing, he lives on–site, as do the two builders and developers of the condos.

 Do you have any policemen or security professionals living there as tenants?

No, we do not. But we encourage everybody, if there's something they don't like, to call the office or call the police, you know, this is a very open policy, because the police certainly want to know and we want to know. I know just the other day, there was somebody that one of the condo people did not think belonged in here, soliciting for some sort of charity, and they called the office and so immediately we said "All right, we'll call the police." So we want to keep it very open, that they can call at any time with any questions. They can either call the police, or, if they think it's a silly question, call up here and we'll call the police.

 And that's a phone line that is strung right into your office.

Our office, right.

 Okay, I will take care of that... So, do the people there have a lot of nice stuff?

It's the high end of the city. You know, as far as condominiums and houses. Except for some of the houses that are up in the hills. We know that, and you will hear it over and over, it's the high end of all condominium projects and high end on the homes.

So you've got a lot of nice cars there? BMW, Mercedes, Lexus?

Yeah, *(laughing)* I'm not a car person, I would say yes, very nice, but my husband always says, "You don't know one car from the other." I know if it's white or red. Had you had a very bad experience in your last gated community?

 You know, it didn't go too well, and a few things happened suddenly that made we want to get out of there fast.

And are you moving here permanently?

 Yes, I did relocate here, and I'm working with a new organization.

Well, if you'd ever like to look... Now I know from our last brochures, we have just sold three homesites within the last week, I don't know what happened, because we are down to nine homesites, and I think maybe, oh, ten condominiums. But if you'd ever like to come out and look at the project, I'd be happy to show you.

 Excellent. And the individual homesites, do those have security systems on them?

It's up to the individual, but in all of our condos we put in full security systems, and I'm sure every home has a full security system.

 Window alarms, closed circuit television systems, what are we talking about here?

All that stuff, yes. I mean, this is just standard when we build the condos. Then the individual can put anything else in, whatever they want.

 But the houses are less fortified?

Well, the security systems in the condos I really am a lot more familiar with, because we have seven builders out here who build the homes, and in the condos we have only one builder, so our offices are at the condos. So, I'm much more familiar with those. But there's full security systems in all of those, and then you may add on anything extra you would want.

Okay. Do you know which of the homes there have the added security?

I would assume absolutely all of them. I mean, it should just be standard nowadays. And what was your last name?

 It's Bradshaw. Yeah, I'd love to come out there sometime and chat with you.

I would love to have you. Our offices are on Prestige Drive, which is the main road for all the homes and condos, it's a big loop. And call us back at this number and ask for me and I'd be happy to take you out and show you what we have.

 And you could show me the different security systems and how the gates work and those kinds of things?

Certainly, I'd be happy to.

 Great. Well, on second thought, I think I have enough information already. Thanks. I should get going now, because I have to come down there and take all your shit.

Hey! Who is thi—(click)

GUN STORE

 Hi, I'm a kindergarten teacher, and I was wondering if I could bring my kindergarten class out to your gun store.

Male Store-Owner: I suppose so.

 I'd like to show them all the wonderful guns that are out there.

Yeah, I think so, but I need a little warning.

 No problem.

Right now I've got the flu so damn bad I didn't talk to anybody that came in today.

 Oh, that's too bad. Sorry to hear that.

So what's your agenda here?

I was hoping that someone there could show the kids the various types of guns that are available, and what they can do. You know, in today's environment I just think that children should be aware of guns, and know how to handle them in case they need to defend themselves in the classroom.

Yeah, what school are you with?

 I'm at JFK Elementary.

Oh, okay. Yeah, if you want to call, maybe next week I'll be a few steps farther from the grave than I am right now.

 Fantastic. Do you have a shooting range there?

No, I don't.

 But you could take the guns apart, show them the difference between regular and armor-piercing ammo, show them how to lock and load—

Yeah, I can illustrate some things.

 Okay. Do you have any guns to fit smaller kids?

You bet.

 Weapons that have less of a kick, they're lighter—

Sure, but I don't know if I'd have anything small enough for a kindergartener.

 Uh-huh, but you have guns for teens and pre-teens?

Oh yeah.

 That's great, they're the ones who really need them. And I'm sure we could find some pistols for the little kids to grow into. So I hope you feel better, buddy.

Yeah, give me a call next week, and if I'm still around, yeah, we can set something up.

 Okay, thanks a lot. The children are very excited to learn more about guns, bullets, and shooting.

ATTORNEY'S OFFICE

 Hi, my name is Mike, and I'm calling you on my cell phone. I'm at a buffet restaurant, and I think I just broke a regulation. I had some salad, then I went up and reused my plate, and it still had some cottage-cheese juice on the plate. Now I'm sitting here and I think I might be in trouble, because I disobeyed what they said on that sign.

Male Attorney: Would you mind telling me a little bit about the sign that you're talking about?

 Sure, it's a sign that says "Please Do Not Re-Use Plates" right by the buffet line.

You're at a buffet right now where this sign is posted?

 I am.

I see. All right, and what is your concern?

 I'm concerned that I flagrantly violated their regulation that they put on their buffet line. I did pay for the buffet, but I also re-used my plate, and I'm thinking they could call the health department on me. I'm wondering if I should get some representation here.

Well, I don't know if this necessarily rises to the level of needing legal representation, but I'll give you what I think. First of all, when you went in there, to be a patron, they could probably argue that the rules were posted and you knew what the rules were. Now, there are two types of rules that you can have. One would be the rule that perhaps they are expressing with this sign, which is also a health ordinance. That would mean something, if there was a city health ordinance that said that you absolutely may not do this.

 Oh, boy.

Now, if it's just their own private rule that they don't want you to do this, and what essentially they're trying to do is just embarass you into having to get a fresh plate so that you might be reminded that you're making a pig of yourself, you are just dealing with their own private rule. Now, the question is, did you necessarily get into a contractual relationship with these people when you did this? In other words, did your behavior create a contract? They offered the food, you accepted it, you paid for it, and they made the rules. Now conceivably, if their public relations department was being run by Adolf Hitler, perhaps they would go after you. However, it doesn't seem as though they would be going after you under normal circumstances. They might politely say, "Excuse me, but we'd prefer that you take a new plate," and then hand you a new plate. But I don't think that there's any problems, this is just one of their rules.

 Okay, let me talk for a second—

If, on the other hand, it's a city ordinance, the question is, who's the ordinance going to be enforced against. Is it going to be enforced against them for permitting you to do this, or is it going to be enforced against you for doing it? And to be perfectly honest, I have not heard of any dirty-plate police having been put into service lately. There might be health inspectors there that might say something about it and have an issue about it—

 Do you think that I should try to get out of here without being noticed? Or do you think I should pile some more food on my plate to hide the fact that it was already dirty?

Well, describe for me a little bit the state of the plate right now.

 Well, as I said, I do have some cottage-cheese juice and some other liquid remnants of my salad here, and that is around the perimeter of the plate. Heaviest concentration between three and seven o'clock. In the middle of the plate I have a pork chop, so that could be suspect, having the pork chop surrounded by the cottage-cheese remnants. I believe those two foods are not usually served together. I just don't want to be trapped in a lie.

Well, do you see people hovering around you now eyeing you suspiciously?

 There is one guy, I think he works here, he's over by the corn. He looks pretty serious.

Is this a place where tipping is allowed, despite the fact that it's a buffet?

 Yeah, I'm sure I could tip.

Well, if this guy can see you, just leave a big tip and I don't think he'll say a word. That's the practical solution. From a legal standpoint, I doubt that they are going to be doing anything in particular where you're concerned, because they probably would have come over if the guy is looking at you now. I mean, you have to take a practical look at this. This is something that most lawyers will never tell you, but there's a practical side of it, too. Odds are, what they want to do is make the place as sanitary as possible. So therefore, they're telling you, take a clean plate, maybe that's for your own benefit as well as for theirs. The other thing is, they might just want to have you somewhat aware of the number of plates that you've taken. Is this an all-you-can-eat buffet, by the way?

 It is.

Well, they ought to be pretty used to people just sidling up to the trough by now. I hope that I have been of some help to you.

 Oh, I certainly do appreciate your verbosity.

Is the food any good?

 It's heavenly.

Well, good luck with this, I don't think you're going to have any real serious legal problems, that's the first thing, and secondly, if there is a Board of Health violation, I think it's going to fall onto the shoulders of the people who are involved with the violation, notably the people that own the restaurant. And the other thing is, that you just shouldn't let this entire incident interfere with your digestion.

 Sir, wait a minute. The corn guy is coming over here right now! I think he has the manager with him!

That's ridiculous.

 I know, I know!

Calm down, sir. What's the address of this restaurant? I can drive over there right now.

SECURITY FIRM

 Hello, I'm in need of some armed security guards.

Male Receptionist: Okay.

Could your company provide me with that service?

We could, but I'd have to put you on the line with Frank. Hang on.

(on hold)

Frank: Hello, this is Frank D'Amato.

 Hi, my name is Mike Loew, and I'm the president of Loewtech, a computer chip manufacturer in Los Angeles. I'm calling because we have a problem here. We had a big contract with a Japanese firm that was supplying us with materials, but we had to terminate that contract when we found out that their firm had ties to organized crime syndicates in Japan.

Oh, I see.

 What I'm worried about is that they might try to send some agents to infiltrate our offices to steal information, or possibly to take revenge upon people here.

Okay sir, what is your address?

 Sure, it's *(provides address)*.

(repeats back address) and what is your name again, sir?

 Mike Loew.

I will come out there myself with a detective and I will talk to you personally.

 What I'm worried about is that they might have some very skilled agents, possibly even ninja-style people. Do you have security officers that are trained in unarmed combat or dealing with potentially dangerous professional ninjas?

We're a full-service private detective agency and security unit. Our private security officers that work here for what we call assert detail, which is what we would classify this as, are security officers that have had law-enforcement training, and quite significant training at that. It goes as far as tactical training. A lot of them are card-toting, deputized police officers that are working off-duty. So as far as that level of expertise and training, we probably have the highest level that you're going to find in the region. Why don't I come on over, I'm going to pull another detective with me, I'll probably be over there in about twenty to twenty-five minutes.

 Oh.

And give me a return telephone number, too.

 Sure, it's *(provides number).*

And what was the firm you were doing business with?

 Fujiwamatsumoto International Technology Systems.

Oh, that's a mouthful.

 They also make a vibrating massage tool that you slip over your fingertip.

Okay, I'll be out in about twenty minutes.

 Uh, great.

SAME SECURITY FIRM

 Hi, this is Mike. I was just talking to you a second ago.

Frank D'Amato: Yes, Mike.

 Actually, you don't want to come down here. These ninjas are way too scary.

Excuse me?

 Seriously, I've seen these guys in action, they can jump forty feet in the air, they can spit spiked metal balls out of their mouth, they are really bad-ass.

Sir, there's a difference between the movies and real life.

 In this case, actually, there's not.

And you want to try and handle these people yourself?

I've gotten myself into this, Frank, and by God, I'll get myself out.

I would not recommend that, sir. We can provide trained security officers that are capable of dealing with threats such as these.

 No, actually, I don't think you can. Have you ever faced a ninja before?

No, not personally, but—

 They are unstoppable killing machines. I was out at the Fujiwamatsumoto headquarters once in Tokyo, and they had their ninjas cleaning up the office there, and you could just tell by the way they swiftly and efficiently vacuumed that they are not to be trifled with.

Sir, our assert detail officers are fully armed, fully equipped personnel with the training—

 No, the only person that can help me now is the White Dragon.

What?

 He is the only ninja that fights on the side of good American corporations, not evil Japanese ones. He's got this awesome white uniform and he totally kicks ass.

This is crazy.

 You got that right. I am OUT THERE, MAN! Forget that you ever even heard of me.

Wanted for aggravating verbal assault and prankery, Mike Loew is now the target of a nationwide manhunt conducted by numerous state and federal law enforcement agencies. So if you have a couch that he could crash on, that would be cool.

HAIR RESTORATION CLINIC

 Hi, my name is Michelle Loew, and I'm calling from my natural foods co-op. All the other women here have long, luxurious hair under their arms, but my body hair is very sparse. I feel like I'm not really fitting in with my coworkers, so I want a nice, thick crop of armpit hair. Can you help me?

Hair Restoration Clinic: No, Dr. Kasparek offers men and women hair restoration for genetic hair loss on the scalp. We offer no other type of treatment, and basically if that's the way your body is growing hair, that's the way it's going to do it. That's just your genetic makeup.

 Do you think I could use some Rogaine on my armpits?

Rogaine is indicated for the genetic hair loss, to help stimulate those hair follicles to not be affected by genetics and to continue to produce hair.

 I see. So you only deal with genetic—

Scalp hair loss, correct.

 It's not so much a cosmetic treatment, but a genetic one?

Correct. It's a cosmetic treatment, but only for the genetic hair loss.

 Okay, but what if I'm suffering genetic hair loss underneath my arms?

If that's the way you're producing hair, that's the way you're producing hair. Everyone produces hair on their body differently. And there's really nothing you can do to change those genetics.

 So, basically, your business has no reason for existing.

I'm sorry, I don't think we can help you. Have a nice day.

HEART TO
HEART

As technological innovations push the human species ever farther from its natural state, our ability to court and mate with sexual partners becomes increasingly stunted and deformed. Happily, there are companies that can help—but their advertising claims must be rigorously tested to protect today's lonely consumer. For the benefit of single adults everywhere, Mike Loew straps on his hands-free telephone headset and looks for love on the line.

WARNING: This chapter contains mature situations and is rated "R" for Raunch. Readers under 18 should tear out the next 33 pages and hide them under their mattresses.

1-900 ADULT PHONE LINE

Female Phone Sex Worker: Mmm, hello?

 Uh, uh, uh, urrrrrrgggGAAAAHHH!!! Whoo, that was great. Thanks.

No, wait baby! *(click)*

DATING SERVICE

 Greetings. They call me Mike Loew.

Female Representative: Hi there, Mike! Tell me, have you ever looked into a dating service before?

 No, you are the first that I have contacted.

And what is prompting you to call us today?

 Well, I have a lifestyle where I don't meet a whole lot of women. I've been into Advanced Dungeons & Dragons for over twenty years now, plus I do a lot of live adventure role-playing. So I'm looking for a woman who's ready to go on a legendary quest with me.

Oh, okay.

 Do you have any women who are involved in Dungeons & Dragons, or who enjoy making their own armor?

Uh, not really. We do have a few women who have said that that is an interest for them, but anybody who's diehard into it, I would say no.

 Any women who watch "Xena," who might want to emulate that medieval ideal of warrior womanhood?

No, to be honest with you, we don't really concentrate on anything specific like that. We look more for the whole picture, looking for somebody for a long-term relationship. We wouldn't really specifically match based on one criteria.

 You don't match people according to their character classes?

Well, we do, but it wouldn't be solely on that. We'd also be looking at other things that you enjoy doing, look at the qualities that you're looking for, so we wouldn't be able to guarantee that that would be something we would be able to match you with, only because it is so specific. No, I don't think we would be able to do that.

 Once again, I am stymied by my passion.

Have you been looking at other services out there? I don't know if anybody else does specific searches like that either. Have you tried the Internet? That might be a good way.

 Ah, yes, the trusty old Internet. Do you think I could find women online that would be into medieval fantasy roleplaying?

I would think so, if you accessed a site like that, that might be a way to do that. Only because that way, that would be a main interest and that would be something that they would enjoy doing. That, and just knowing from my membership pool, I don't think that we have very many women that are into that stuff very much.

 Well, hey, besides just the gaming, you know, I do a lot of other things. I like to brew mead—

I didn't hear what you said.

 Oh, I brew mead, it's a medieval beverage. I'm a musical soul as well, I enjoy playing my lute and recounting my most glorious adventures in rhymed couplets.

Okay, okay. Are you working?

 I'm a full-time gamer.

Oh, you get paid to do that?

 Yes, I test out games for various companies and run players through the adventure modules. I'm a professional dungeonmaster.

How interesting.

 I'm known throughout the industry as one of the toughest dungeonmasters working today.

Well, that's really interesting, I have not heard of that before. So you are doing that full-time.

You bet. Also, I travel around to all the gaming conventions and figure–painting competitions—hey, that's another thing I do, I paint little miniature figures, so I do have other—

Wait, you said you paint figures or finger–painting?

 No, miniature fantasy figurines.

Oh, I thought, "You do finger-painting competitions? Wow, that's kind of interesting!" *(laughs)*

 Ha ha, no. It's more the small lead dragons, elves, orcs, dwarves, skeletons, goblins, hobgoblins, wizards, kobolds, knights, ogres, dark elves—

I know what you're talking about, my boyfriend plays, so—

 Oh, really?

Yup. He—

 Do you two ever run through an exciting adventure together?

Um, I do not. I know a little about the card games—I know they're all different. He plays with cards and he has miniatures that he plays with, other than that, that's about it. I get kicked out of the house once a month and all the guys come over!

 Do they need an experienced dungeonmaster?

I'm not sure—they don't do anything where they do the live reenactments. I know he has a few friends that do, but that's not something that he does, so I'm not very familiar with it at all. But my cousins play Pokémon, so I know that's a little bit like it!

 Is he a pretty good figure painter? I'd love to take a look at his miniatures sometime.

Oh, he loves it. To be honest with you, I don't know what would be considered good. I really don't, unfortunately it's one of those things where I'm not artistic, so if you can basically get it to all be one color, I'm thinking that's pretty good!

 So he doesn't do any drybrushing techniques to pick out the highlights on the individual links of chain mail?

I'm not necessarily the best person to make that judgment call, but if you want to, what you could do, Mike, is fill out that brochure that you got and send it back in, and what we could do then is be able to see how many people that we would have that would be compatible with you. And then from there we would be able to tell you whether this is something worthwhile for you to do. But that would be one way to go about it.

Okay, but maybe your boyfriend could help me out. If he's involved with gaming, and he's involved with you, that gives me a lot of hope. Does he game with any women in the area?

You know, I'm not sure, I know he only plays with gentlemen. Geez, I really don't know. I mean, if he has questions and stuff he has in the past gone online and found out some answers, so I know that there are a few people out there that do it. But other than that... When you do a lot of your work, you don't meet any women that way?

You know, not a whole lot, to tell you the truth. Usually it's men who are involved with the little figurines and graph paper and dice. Yeah, women are a little scarce at the gaming conventions.

Yeah, I could see that.

Except for this one woman that I saw at Gen-Con back in '89. She was wearing a Car Wars T-shirt. She was so beautiful.

Okay, if you want to, definitely send that brochure in, and if anything comes up, I'd be happy to keep you on file.

Sure, I will do that. Could I enclose a few photos of some of the things that I do, like some of the miniatures that I paint and some of my best costumes?

If you want to. It's not necessary.

Okay, just to have those resources on file for some lucky lady to check out?

You certainly could do that. All right?

Great. Look for those in your snail mail.

Okay, thanks, Mike.

KINKY COEDS 1-900 LINE

(Synthesized funk groove intro)

Recorded Kinky Coed: Mmmm, ohh, oh, please don't stop, please, yes, you feel so good, ohh, oh I'm not finished yet, mmm, ahh, my girlfriends and I are waiting so impatiently, mmm, and we need it baaaad. Let me tell you, you've come to the best live phone service, mmm, where you can hear the most outrageous, the most daring, and the dirtiest live campus action, ohh, lover, my girlfriends and I are waiting, ohhhh, for you, mmm, oh, this is the best phone sex you'll ever have, our coeds are waiting to give it to you live, to caress your throbbing body with our soft and able hands, mmm, we've got it all for you, just the way you like it, oh, I'm wet and ready for you, my pussy is aching and it needs relief, oh, one of the very special girls in our dorm is Susan, she's a real angel, she likes guys, she likes girls, Susan likes to have fun, Susan has looong legs, and she likes to give guys a good time, she has beautiful lips, and she sure knows how to use them! So are you ready to do it live? Are you ready to do it like never before? Oh, I bet you are. Baby, stay on the line and don't go anywhere else. I want you to fuck me live, really hard, so don't be shy, stay with me, let's study each other's—*(beep)*

Live Kinky Coed: Hello?

 Hey, this is college coeds?

No, sweetheart, this is not college. What college are you looking for?

 Oh, this isn't the college coed line?

No, sweetheart, this is a hot fantasy line.

 Hey, it says college coeds in the ad.

Sweetheart, you've got the wrong number. You need to hang up and call back and listen to the hot sex I have. What, you want to register for a course?

 No, I was looking for some help on my term paper, actually.

Oh, you were looking for some help on your term paper. I'll give you some help on your ass.

On my ass? I really don't have time for that right now, whatever "that" might be. I'm working on a big term paper on Imperial Russia.

Oh, you're working on a term paper on Imperial Russia? Why don't I give you a term paper on Imperial Russia's ass? Or his cock?

 His cock? Huh, there's not a whole lot about that in my notes. I just saw the ad with the college girl, and I really need some help—

On Imperial Russia, they talk about ass, cock, dick, suck, everything. I could give you a little, or I could fuck you over how to suck a cock. That's what you want to do, baby, learn how to suck a cock?

 Who, me? No, not really, all I'm thinking about is getting this term paper done.

Okay, so what if I do a term paper on your ass, baby?

 I don't get it, a term paper on my ass. How does that work? I need to get my notes together, I need to get it down on the paper—

Okay, no problem, baby, you just talk to me, you just kiss my ass and let me fuck you up yours.

 What is wrong with you? The ad says it's a coed line, and girls always take better notes than me, so I thought—

No, sweetheart, it's a fantasy porno line for fuck.

 Is English your first language? Where are you located?

I'm located in the island of New Zealand, sweetheart.

 Okay, so do you know anything at all about Imperial Russia?

Yes, sweetheart, I know about Russia's ass.

 You mean Siberia?

Sweetheart, I'm just kidding, I can't help you with your bookwork, this is a fantasy line. We only have sex, make love, fuck on this line. I'm sorry, I'm just kidding with you. I don't know nothing about your bookwork. Imperial Russia? I don't even know who that is.

All right. Is there anyone else there who's an actual coed that could tell me something about the Decembrist revolt in 1825?

No, sweetheart, the only thing people here could do is suck your cock and teach you how to suck a cock.

Faint Man's Voice: Yeah.

Kinky Coed: And fuck a ass. Okay, sweetheart?

 Well, that's really too bad...

Slightly Louder Man's Voice: Yeah.

 Hey, who's that guy?

Kinky Coed: I have someone else, baby, it's a party line, it's not a college.

 Hey, I party on the weekends, but I totally have to get this done by noon on Friday.

Okay, sweetheart, tell you what you do, you call me back on the weekend, okay? I wish you all the luck with your homework, and I hope you get it done, okay? 'Bye, honey, have a nice day.

 Thanks.

You're welcome.

DATING SERVICE FOR PROFESSIONALS

 My name is MIKE LOEW!

Female Representative: Well, hello, Mike!

 Your service helps out busy professionals, RIGHT?!?

Exactly. I'm the director here, my name's Vicki, and I'll tell you all about it! I'm working with about a thousand clients in the metropolitan area—busy professionals working long hours, who don't want to go to bars to meet people, things like that. So they come to me! Tell me what you do, Mike.

I am a PROFESSIONAL WRESTLER!

Excellent! Now, tell me how long you've been doing that.

 I have spent FIVE BLOODY YEARS in the RING!

How do you like it?

 Things are going WELL! The field is changing EVERY DAY! But it has been difficult... I'm on the road a lot, and it's hard to meet people, so I just wanted to meet that special someone who could share my love of WRESTLING!

Sure! So do you travel just all the time?

 I am on the road QUITE A BIT! BUT—I have my own TRAILER, it has my NAME and LOGO on the SIDE—it's VERY NICE!

Well, we're nationwide. So if you are travelling, and you're in another city, you can always date there too. We can set something up wherever you are, if you're interested in that.

 LET'S DO IT!

Okay, I will be doing all the matching for you. So the first thing that would happen is we would sit down and talk for about an hour, and we're going to go over everything that you're looking for. Talk about your last girlfriend, things that you love, and things that you want me to focus on with your matching.

 THE ONE THING THAT I AM FOCUSED ON IS WINNING THE WORLD CHAMPIONSHIP BELT! You know, in addition to having a relationship with someone special.

All right, so those are the things we would talk about. What your hopes are, and what you find attractive, and everything. Basically, if I think I can match you, that's when you'll join. And it's a year, or at least twelve dates, whichever comes first, for a thousand dollars. You're hiring me as your personal assistant.

 Are you up to the CHALLENGE of personally assisting HOMO DESTRUCTUS?!?

Homo Destructus?

That's my stage name. I'm like a huge caveman that was frozen in a glacier, and then got thawed out by scientists, and now I've returned to civilization to wrestle. Have you seen my ACTION FIGURE?!?

No, I don't think I have.

 I run around in a LOINCLOTH on the MAT, I wear animal-tooth NECKLACES, but it's all an ACT! I'm really just a NICE FAMILY GUY!

Absolutely! Well, I'd love to meet you and set up an interview, and we can get started from there.

HORNY ASIANS 1-900 LINE

Recorded Horny Asian: Oh, baby, me so horny all the time. I need big stud like you who likes horny, kinky Oriental girls that like to sucky-sucky and bangy-bangy all night long! I know horny stud like you want name and phone number of beautiful, erotic Oriental girls that live near you! Or, you can talk live to me and all my hot and horny Oriental girlfriends, and we teach you the secrets of the Orient. I promise you not be disappointed! If you do not have a credit card, please press the star key for direct access into our system, brought to you by Phonecom International—*(beep)*

Live Horny Asian: Hello?

 Hi, is this a horny Asian?

Oh yeah, you know me horny for you.

 That's why I'm calling today. The overpopulation crisis in Asia is due in large part to horny Asians like yourself. Are you aware of the current population densities in Asian countries?

Mmm, yeah, baby.

 Japan has a population density of 336 people per square kilometer, Bangladesh has 952.9, and the Chinese territory of Macao has an astonishing 24,143 people per square kilometer—

Oh, baby, me not know such stuff. Me only want to sucky-sucky and humpy-humpy. You want a little humpy-humpy, baby?

No, that's exactly the kind of behavior that is leading to such problems in Asia. With more and more people crammed into limited land space, child malnutrition rates are rising, infant mortality is rising, life expectancy is dropping amongst the general population—

You a teacher or something?

 No, I'm just a concerned citizen of the planet Earth. Now, what are you going to do about the overpopulation crisis in Asia?

What can I do? I am no president of Asia. I just wait here for you to call because me want your big strong cock.

 Okay, I realize that horny habits are hard to break, but I'm going to give you some very important advice, all right?

Oh yeah, baby, you tell me what you want me to do.

 First, always use a condom, even during phone sex.

Condom, yeah, me put condom on you for fucky-fucky.

 Second, limit yourself to monogamous relationships. There are too many people in Asia to have sex with.

Mmm, yeah, me have sex all the time.

 And finally, try to develop interests and hobbies outside of "humpy-humpy" and "bangy-bangy," such as origami, kung fu, or tea ceremonies. All right?

Okay, we do tea ceremony and I wear long silk kimono, okay? And then I drop kimono and me all naked for you, okay? Then we drink tea and do humpy at same time. You like that, big horny man?

 Ma'am, you are the horny Asian, not me. Now please try to control yourself. Your continent needs you.

1-900 ADULT PHONE LINE

Setting: the sparkling headquarters of The Onion, America's Finest News Source. The award-winning staff of Onion writers warm up their vocal chords while Mike Loew takes out his credit card.

 Mmm, I am so ready to enter all sixteen digits of my VISA number.

 John Krewson: Please enter the first four digits of your card now... now... NOW!

 Tim Harrod: Oh, keep entering it!

 Rob Siegel: Mmm, your credit card number is so good...

 Todd Hanson: You guys, quit with the wisecracks, come on now.

 Why? We can control ourselves. We can handle our cracks.

 You're making it harder for me. You're making me laugh.

 That's your cross to bear.

 Phone sex is always just about you, isn't it?

 You're just so selfish. *(pause)* So what were you saying, John?

 Enter it harder! HARDER!

 Shhh, okay, here we go.

 (pulls hat down over head) Oh, Christ.

 (into phone) Hello? Hi, my name is Mike, and I'm here with a few of my good friends. We all need some phone sex, but we really need to save some money, too, so can I put you on speaker phone? Would that be okay? Great, hold on one sec. Hello? Ma'am?

Female Phone Sex Worker: Thanks for calling Hot College Pussy!

 No problem! Hey, I just put you on speaker phone.

What?

 I was just talking to you, I put you on speaker phone.

I was not just talking to you.

 Oh, sorry, my name's Mike and I'm here with some buddies of mine because we wanted to save some money on the phone sex. So I've got Todd and John and Rob and Tim and myself here, and we're ready for some hot phone action.

Are you guys gay?

 No way!

 Hey, c'mon!

 Jesus!

I am sorry, okay, you guys may be, like, different, but me and my girlfriends, we don't sit around and play with ourselves if we're not, like, sexually involved with each other, you know what I mean?

 Hey, this is just about the phone.

(indignantly) O-kay.

 You know, it's just really expensive, and we're trying to save money.

It is expensive, isn't it?

 We're not all rich like you college types.

Whaaat?

 We have to work for our money.

I still don't see why we would call a college girl if we were gay.

Did you say I was rich? Did you just imply that I have money? Man, if I had money I would not be working here.

 What's your dream job?

To be a pimp. Wouldn't that be phat?

 Do they have programs for that in college?

Huh?

 Do they teach that in college?

No, I don't think so. I would be, like, the first to sign up!

 Maybe UNLV.

Aww, you don't need to learn much about pimpin'.

 Hey, pimpin' ain't easy. But back to the phone sex. We need to get that going—

Right—

 —because we're not gay. We just do a lot of things together.

I hear ya.

 Our phone bills have been murder. I mean, it's really hard to afford.

I know it is! You don't have to tell me that.

 I just need a little love.

So you're going to kill five birds with one stone?

 Yeah, that's what we're trying to do.

Some big birds.

Big birds?

 It's just that we each spend, on average, six, seven hundred dollars a month on phone sex, and we figured we could—

Oh my God! What about real sex?

 Real sex?

 We can't afford that.

 That is even more expensive, believe me.

You don't have to pay for sex!

 Well, we do, but we realized that if we all got together and did it, we could split the cost.

 We're not even looking at each other. We're sitting in a circle with our backs to the phone, facing away from each other.

You know, you guys are the ones that are stuck on this. I accept it. I understand.

 Great! Let's get naked.

(peevishly) Okay, well, you guys tell me what you're into. I'm not psychic. I'd be working for LaToya if I was psychic. I'd be a psychic friend. So what do you guys like?

 Uh, nudity?

 Girls.

 Chicks!

What do you look like?

I'm 5'7", I weigh about 120, I have black hair, green eyes, my measurements are 32-22-32, I have a D-cup, I'm nineteen—

Wait a minute, that is such a coincidence, because the last person I talked to had those same measurements, and they were also a D-cup, and they were nineteen!

No, because the last girl you talked to was Dylan, because she's sitting right by me. She was like, "I cannot deal with the speaker phone!"

So you two are just hanging out in your cubicle, chatting about sex, just like us!

Pretty much. But see, the thing that is different is that I'll eat her pussy—you guys won't suck each others' cocks. That's why it's different, that's what I was trying to explain. It's different when it comes to girls, if we're going to be together, getting ourselves off, it's gonna end up to be getting each other off.

That's a crazy coincidence, actually, because our friend Carol just walked in. Hey, Carol!

Carol Kolb: Hi. What the hell are you guys doing?

Oh, we're just saving some money on phone sex.

Oh, cool! Who is that on the phone?

(under her breath) An actress.

Well, I don't usually do it with girls, but that's cool, I could try. That would be new.

Well...

So let's get it on.

Right, we're wasting too much time here.

 Yeah, the meter's running.

(*peeved again*) What?

 We've probably already spent a good twelve dollars each already, so we've gotta—

 Yeah, we should get going. Is your pussy wet yet?

My pussy is, I've been here since fuckin' nine this morning, of course it's wet.

 Good God!

There's nothing else to do except play with myself all day, ha ha, so it's wet.

 Well, that's a good start.

 No kiddin'!

 My cock is not all that hard right now for some reason.

 Yeah, I'm working on it too, but it's not quite there yet...

Jack it off, or something—

 Would you guys please hurry your asses up? It's always like this with them. I'm sitting here, I've been ready ever since you said hello.

 What's your name?

My name? Arden. Like arden without a "g," or Elizabeth Arden.

Elizabeth Arden, sure. Well, I don't know about these guys, their cocks aren't hard yet—

 I'm hard! I didn't say I wasn't hard!

 Well, Mike said his isn't hard, but mine is hard, this is Rob, hi, hi Arden, um, I'd like you to start sucking my cock, if you don't mind.

I love sucking dick.

 If these guys aren't ready yet, please, I want you to go down on me.

 Rob also has dark hair, he has beautiful brown eyes, he's about 5'11"—

I don't need to know all that.

 Anyway, he's sitting, so if you could get on your knees while you suck him, then I could get going from behind here.

You know what, though? Here's the problem. When I suck dick, I have to have the guy fuck my mouth. So I have to be on my knees, and he's gotta be standing up, shoving it down my throat.

 Okay, but what if I was lying on the floor then and you straddled me?

That would work!

 Excellent!

 Now we're getting somewhere!

 Hey, this is John, and since I'm hard and these guys obviously aren't—

 Oogh! Hey, speak for yourself.

I'm going to enter you from behind then. Right behind you here.

 Wait a minute, I'm confused, because Tim said he was already entering her from behind.

 No, she explained—

No, listen! I will work this out for you guys, okay, how many of there are you?

 Wait, she's working it out! Just let her talk! She's the professional.

How many of there are you?

 We have five guys and one woman.

 Yeah, I'm still here.

 I'll enter from behind while you're talking.

 Arden, what about my cock?

 Will you just LET HER TALK? JESUS!

Thank you. Okay, here's what we're going to do. Um, the girl?

 Yeah?

You? Okay, you lie on your back.

 Okay, I can see that. With my legs spread, or—

I'm going to be on my hands and knees in a sixty-nine position, okay? And one of you guys fuck me in my pussy from behind, and—

 Well, that's what I was gonna do, but you said it was impossible because you're blowing Rob, or having him "fuck your mouth."

Wait a second—are you ready?

 Yeah, I'm ready!

Okay, Carol, is that your name?

 Yeah.

Okay, you can lick my pussy and suck his cock while he fucks me, well, not really his cock, but you know, like lick his balls or whatever? And then one of you can kind of go over to the side on your knees—

 Why are we paying you for Carol to suck Rob's cock when they're both here?

 We can give Carol twelve bucks later.

 Just let her do her JOB, people!

 Okay, go ahead, I'm fucking your mouth, go ahead.

I have three holes on my body.

 Okay, I got your mouth.

There are five of you guys?

 Well, we can share, we can take turns or whatever, however you want to do it.

 Let's use the buddy system.

I will have a dick in my mouth, but one of you gets to fuck Carol in her pussy, or her ass, whatever you're into.

 Well, again, it seems strange to be paying you money to do that, but whatever, I'll work with it.

Okay, Tim, so hop on Carol—

 Tim, just try to get into it and quit being so critical. Because we're trying to have a good time, and you're bringing a lot of negative energy into the phone sex.

 I didn't mean to, the whole point of this was to save money, all right, I've just got my eye on the bottom line here.

 Okay, Arden, I'm fucking your mouth, this is Rob, Tim is fucking Carol, Carol is, um, what is Carol fucking?

 Carol's going down on Arden.

No, she's lying on her back, basically like—

 Oh, and Arden is squatting on her.

I'm on my hands and knees in a sixty-nine position over her—

 Right, I got it.

So she can kind of lick my clit, and, you know—

 Hey, I like that idea!

 And you're licking hers, right?

 No, it's her mouth that's getting fucked.

 Oh, because I'm fucking your mouth, never mind, sorry.

 Try to concentrate, Rob, geez, you're supposed to be fucking her mouth, you know? Pay attention to what you're doing.

 Okay, so what about John?

I can get probably both of the heads of your cocks in my mouth.

Yeah, John, you do that, because I don't want to be anywhere near Rob's cock. I'm not into that.

If you want to get off, you'll just have to put your inhibitions aside.

 Well, it looks like it's you and me in someone's mouth again, Rob.

 So are the five of us now accounted for? Can we get going on this?

 Yeah, let's just get going, c'mon! My pussy is dripping all over the place!

 Well, I'm not involved yet, but that's fine, I'll just wait my turn.

 How about Todd gets kind of aroused, and he just starts stroking himself while he's watching us.

 Why don't I just touch the breasts or something that is still open. No one's on the breasts yet, right?

 Do you have nice tits?

Do I?

 Yes, you, the phone sex worker.

(rapidly tiring) Yeah, they're nice.

 Yeah, remember, she said they were D-cups.

 Implants?

No. I actually don't like my breasts, just because they're a pain in the ass, you know what I mean?

 That doesn't sound very sexy.

When I was younger and they were big, all the guys were grabbing them and stuff. But they're nice, they're nice.

Okay, that's good. Now guys, try to concentrate, because you're wrecking the mood, and I'm trying to get into this.

 Well, I'm good to go.

 Yeah, I guess, I'm a little fuzzy on my involvement and position, but I'm ready, I'm ready to go with it.

Know what?

 What?

Why don't we do something else.

 (general exasperation from group) **No, we just got this going, we just got it organized!**

I'm just kidding. God.

 Oh, she was kidding, okay.

 You seem like a very nice person, Arden.

Thank you, so do you guys, but you need to learn to talk one at a time.

 Okay, Arden, I just really want to get going because I'm really good to go, I'm hot—

And I want to go home, too.

 —my cock is really hard and throbbing, and I just really want to fuck your mouth.

Okay. So shove it down my throat—

 Okay, there it goes. Ooh.

Okay, here are the conditions.

Yeah?

Shove it down my throat, so I can stick my tongue out and lick your balls, and you have to shoot your cum in my mouth and on my face.

 You're going to swallow it?

(*angrily*) Yeah, I'm going to swallow it! What are you—I can't believe you just asked that question. Of course I'm going to swallow.

 All right, I haven't been with a woman in a few weeks now, so it's going to be a big load.

Ooh, good, perfect.

 You're going to get the whole thing down?

Some on my face, some on my face.

 Just don't get any of it on me.

 Or on me, who's in there with you, by the way.

 I'm just saying, it's going to be a lot of hot, pumping cum.

That's fine.

 Okay, steaming hot cum. Well, I'm hard, and I'm in your mouth right now.

Mmmm...

 Oh, yeah...

 Okay, now Rob, after you're done, can I get in there after you?

 After she swallows all my cum and licks my balls, all right?

Because I'll wait patiently, but—

 Okay, now I'll start fucking you, and pretty soon I want John's cock in your mouth too, all right?

Can I put my finger up you guys' asses?

 Oh, I love that. Could you do that?

I'll stick it in my pussy first, you know, get it nice and wet.

 That's commendable that you're at the end of a long shift but your pussy's still wet. If there's a customer survey to fill out, I'd be glad to mention that.

Oh my god, you don't understand, I knew this guy that went to the hospital because he almost drowned. I was sitting on his face.

 (whistles with amazement)

 Really?

No, I'm lying, but it does get very wet.

 Whew, I was getting nervous about my own safety there.

 Oh, wow. You sound hot.

Thanks.

 I think she sounds hot.

 Absolutely! I wish I weren't over here with Carol.

Why don't you fuck Carol? How are you guys going to let some woman be there and not—

I got a man, I can't fuck him, but I'm going to get myself off over here.

 Oh, super, that works out great for me.

 She's not bisexual, but she's definitely bi-curious.

It's fun. You know what, though? Oh, my God. Once you're with a woman, you will not need these guys.

 Really?

I swear to God.

 But you love cock, don't you? You're going to enjoy sucking my cock, aren't you?

Yeah, I'm just saying, when I first started fucking around with my girlfriends, we were not even looking at guys.

 Oh, God, I know what you mean, women are so hot.

 Wait, I'm losing my erection now.

We're talking about lesbians and you're losing your erection? What is wrong with you?

 No, you said that you didn't look at guys, and that's making me think you don't like men, and that's making me feel sort of rejected, emotionally.

 He wants you to want him.

 Yeah, I just need to feel wanted.

 Oh shit, aww, that's it for me.

Christ, John, I just bought these shoes!

 Okay, I'm in John's place now.

 Let's get it on, Arden, I really wanna—

 It looks like Rob's almost ready to come too. His scrotal sack looks pretty tight.

 Hey, quit looking at Rob! You're gonna wreck the mood!

 Arden, Arden, come on—

 It's hard for me to get in here because I'm a little bigger than John was, but I think I can manage—

 Come on, Arden.

What?

 Come on, suck me. Suck me.

 Oh, God.

Oh my goodness.

 Oh, suck me.

 Oh, yeah.

 Oh, God.

 It's great to see you guys working together like this.

Urgh. Aah. Whoop!

(*aside*) You want to hear this, Dylan?

 Oh, baby.

Can my girlfriend listen?

 Yeah, sure!

 It's a party.

 Will she join in? We could use a couple more holes.

She'll eat my pussy.

 That's good.

 That's great.

All right, let me put you on speaker, okay?

 Definitely bring in the others.

Okay, okay.

 Oh god, and you're sucking me.

(*pause*) Can you hear us?

 Yeah. Is your friend there now?

Yep, got her.

 All right, Arden, Arden, just stay with me, you're sucking me, you're licking my balls, okay?

Can one of you lick my pussy?

I want to lick your pussy.

 All right, lick Carol's, because Carol is hot.

 Wait a minute. If we're both in her mouth, then how can she lick Carol's pussy?

 Let's not worry about that.

 I wish Stephen were here. He's good at figuring out this kind of stuff.

Carol, you don't need real cock.

 Now Carol is shaved, is that okay?

It's perfect.

 Aww, she's like a little girl.

 Yup.

 All this talk about pussy is making me hungry.

Dylan: (to Arden) What the hell is wrong with them, talking about dick and pussy, and they're not fucking around?

Arden: I don't know, I don't know.

 Actually, we're all coworkers, so that really wouldn't be appropriate to lick each other's pussies.

 It wouldn't be good for the workplace environment.

 Come on, Arden, I'm in your mouth, and now what are you going to do? What are you going to do to Tim?

Yeah, get me in here.

 Tim's waiting, how can you accommodate him?

Shove it down my throat.

 Okey-dokey!

 Me and Tim are down your throat.

 Sorry if I'm crowding you, Rob, but I was born that way.

 Do you have any room in that hot, wet cunt for Tim?

Sure.

 Okay, Tim's going to go in your cunt—

 Awesome!

 —and now Mike wants to be in your mouth.

 You know, I have been waiting very patiently here.

 Yeah, Todd has been furtively masturbating in the corner for awhile now.

 I'd be willing to let Todd in on this for a little bit.

 It doesn't have to be Arden, it could be her friend, it could be just about anybody, really...

We have two girls here. Oh, we have three girls here right now.

 What are the other girls' names?

Dylan and Kendall.

Dylan and Kendall—so there's three people there now.

 All right! Sounds good!

 We don't even need you, Carol.

 Let's get an octuple daisy chain going.

 I want Kendall—Kendall, are you there?

Kendall: What the fuck are they—

Arden: Kendall, they're talking to you.

Kendall: What?

 Are you there, Kendall?

Yeah.

 So what do you want to do?

I don't know, how many people are there?

 Just go to work on Todd.

 Just concentrate on me. Don't worry about the others.

 Yeah, let's give her to Todd. Todd's worked hard all week.

 I've been very patient.

I've got Todd? (*all three college girls giggle derisively*)

 Come on, we want you to fuck us.

What do you want me to do?

Just let me get Todd's cock, because I won't suck anything under six.

 Oh, it's a good seven, eight.

 (snorts with suppressed laughter) **Sorry.** *(college girls giggle again)*

 That's when it's flaccid.

 Come on, guys, this is the world of imagination here. I can say however much I want.

Arden: It's hard to imagine something that's not there.

 That does seem to be the central problem here.

 Yeah, it really does.

 You know, maybe this whole phone sex thing wasn't the best idea.

 Hey, I'm having a really good time, you guys.

 I'm digging it!

 Maybe this whole system isn't going to work. Tell you what, I'm just going to concentrate on what Kendall is saying, and just let me have like thirty seconds, and then you guys can join back in.

 Kendall, why don't you do some grunting for Todd.

 No, just describe some scenario that you like, Kendall, it can be whatever you're into.

 Do whatever you want to Todd.

Arden: How many of you have come? Any of you?

Only one.

Jesus Christ.

 Well, whose fault is that?

 John came, didn't you, John?

 I'm back up again.

 I'm a little nervous.

 I'm ready to come, I just need a little help. *(the college girls hang up)* Hello? Hello? Oh, that's just great. How am I supposed to have an orgasm now?

Mike Loew is available for appearances at Tough Call book-burning parties.

SERB FEST

Female Receptionist: St. Nikola Cathedral.

 Hi there, I noticed in the Yellow Pages here that you guys are in charge of Serb Fest.

Uh, yeah?

 I'm just curious if we're still planning on doing that this year.

Uh, for next year. August. Yeah, August twenty... ooh, I don't have the dates right now, right in front of me, I had them about a minute ago... *(trails off into a whisper)*

 I have the dates, it says August 27th to the 29th, which is a great weekend for me. I'm really looking forward to it, but was just curious if the fair is still going to happen in light of the recent events.

Oh, yes, we're having people... It's 25th, 26th, and 27th.

 Okay, great. So will there be any Albanians there? I'm a Serbo-American myself, and I was just curious if there were going to be any Albanians there.

Well, I don't know, it's a festival. You mean, as far as, participating?

 Yeah.

What, as dance groups?

 Well, I was just hoping that there wouldn't be any there, actually.

Well, I don't know, if they come to participate in the festival, we don't know who, and if they don't say, "We're Albanian," ha ha, we won't know who's Albanian and who's not.

 Weird. So you could be hanging out with Albanians and you wouldn't even know?

It's open to the public, yah, but I doubt that they would attend. But it's open for the public, people can, anybody can attend.

Okay, so is there going to be any American flag burning going on? I built a nice papier-mâché effigy of President Clinton, actually, and I was hoping to burn that at the festival.

No, that isn't allowed, we would never allow that to happen here.

 Oh, there's no flag burning planned at all?

No, why would we want to do that?

 Just because America bombed the Serbs so ferociously.

That would be something that would be illegal to do here, and I don't think that we would do that. We've established ourselves as a community here for many years, and we would never, ever do something like that.

 Oh, okay.

And we wouldn't encourage anybody to do that either.

 So you don't think I would be able to do that there?

No, I don't think so.

 Okay. Will there be any fireworks?

No, we don't have fireworks.

 So what's on tap for Serb Fest this year? What do you have planned?

Well, it's a folk festival, it's ethnic food, ethnic dancing—

 Ethnic cleansing?

Ethnic dancing.

 Oh, okay.

Are you Serbian?

 Yes, I'm a Serbo-American.

You are.

Yup.

Why are you talking about ethnic cleansing?

 Oh, just because that's what the Serbs are into, right?

Oh really? And you're Serbian and you're telling me that Serbs are doing this?

 Sure.

Why would you have that attitude, then?

 Oh, just because that's what Milosevic said he was doing to the Muslim population in Bosnia and Kosovo.

Well, if you believe that, that's in your heart what you believe, um, you can... Milosevic is saying that?

 Yeah, isn't that what the Serbian government said they wanted to do, to cleanse the Albanians out of Kosovo?

I think you might be Albanian and you're talking to me. You're Serbian?

 Yeah, I'm Serbian, I'm no Albanian. I totally hate those guys! So you don't think that Milosevic was in favor of ethnic cleansing?

I'm sorry, I don't talk about political things, this is a church office, okay? Good-bye.

 All right. Viva la Serbia!

THE DRUG WAR

The scourge of drug abuse continues to tear apart our nation's moral fabric. Yet with employee drug testing, highly militarized national borders, and a Drug Czar appointed to fight drugs on a federal level, America has not surrendered the battle against dangerous narcotics. Mike Loew speaks to a number of soldiers in The Drug War in order to gain insights about their work and their mission.

COUNCIL ON DRUG ABUSE

 Hi, I'm calling from Los Angeles because I have a young son, and recently I've come to think that my son is using marijuana.

Female Councillor On Drug Abuse: Okay.

 I'm worried about this, so last night I asked him to show me his bag of pot. Then, to foster a sense of communication and openness, our family all smoked it together. I was calling to see if you think that's a good approach to the problem.

What did he have?

 He probably had about a quarter-ounce of fresh, leafy marijuana, and we smoked it in his smooth, cool water bong.

And that was to show him...

 I had never done it before, so I wanted to make sure he's not in over his head.

Have you noticed any changes in him? What made you suspicious?

 Well, he's been awfully creative lately. He's been drawing a lot, writing poetry, and playing in a rock and roll band.

Is that new behavior for him?

 He was a bit dull before. There's the upsurge in creativity, and he's been having more of a social life. And I could smell a funny smell coming from his room, along with laughter and general merriment.

That's very common, they'll often burn incense to cover up the smell of marijuana, because it has a very distinct odor. Can I have your first name?

 Sure, it's Mike. But do you think that was a good idea, to smoke it with him? I'm looking for some guidance here, because he's making plans to invite some people over and smoke tonight with me again.

I would not encourage smoking with your son. How old is he?

 Eight.

I would not encourage that. I hear that you're wanting openness and communication, but the message that's also sending is it's okay to use this illegal substance, as long as we use it together. I think you need to be careful what kind of messages you send to him.

We do a lot of things together, my son and I. We enjoy fishing, camping and boating. But ever since he started smoking marijuana, we haven't been doing those things so much, so I thought I should see what he's up to lately. I like to think of myself as kind of hip, for a dad. Have you ever smoked marijuana?

Yes.

What do you think about it?

I think it's very psychologically addicting. Even the things you've talked about—the creativity, the sociability—you can become psychologically dependent on marijuana to help you be those things. So if someone says, "A bunch of us are getting together for a party this weekend," you think, "Oh my gosh, now I've got to get some marijuana so I can smoke up before I go to this party, so I can be social."

Or you could bring it to the party and let everyone smoke it. That would be fun.

He could, but then if he got caught he'd be in a lot of trouble.

Am I in trouble for smoking last night?

I would discourage you from doing that with him again. I'm going to give you the phone number of a treatment center that deals exclusively with children and their families. What you may want to do is contact them, and have a family session with someone there.

Do you think we could smoke it there?

No, this is a treatment center.

Oh, yeah, okay.

This is a treatment center. Why would you want to smoke it there? I would encourage you, before you get involved with this, to get more information, both for yourself and for your son. Your son is eight years old, he is undergoing some very important developmental changes, and smoking or doing drugs can interfere with those processes. I'm going to give you this number—*(provides number)*. They can assess where your son is at with his marijuana usage, and answer any questions you might have, too. Are there any other questions that you have for me?

 Do you think that when a person smokes marijuana, the seeds should be separated from the leaves, or should they just be mixed in with the rest of the stuff?

Is this for you or for your son, that you're asking this?

 Both of us were a little confused about this.

Okay, I don't know that I can give you any advice about that, but I can recommend that you get some guidance from people who work specifically with children. For your interest, and it sounds pretty strong, I would also encourage you to get some education on it before you develop a dependency on it.

 What are the dangers that come with repeated usage, besides the enhanced creativity and social life?

Certainly it can affect your lungs, it can affect your memory; you can become psychologically dependent on it to be social, to be creative—you can depend on it just to function, psychologically. You won't suffer physical withdrawal symptoms from it, but you'll suffer mentally and emotionally if you become addicted to it.

 Hey, my son's friends just got here. Thanks, gotta go.

Mm-hmm. Thank you and good luck.

DARE

 Hello, my name is Mike Loew, and I'm calling from Los Angeles. I'm a neighborhood, street corner-style drug pusher, and frankly, I'm a little tired of all the negative publicity that DARE has been perpetuating about what we do.

Female DARE Representative: A neighborhood drug pusher?

 Right. I'm proud of my profession, and—*(DARE hangs up)* Hello?

DRUG TESTING SERVICE

 Hello, I'm calling from Los Angeles. Can I speak with someone in charge of drug testing?

Male Drug Tester: That's me.

 This is Mike Loew. I'm the chief executive officer of LoewCorp Incorporated.

Okay.

 I'm calling because we recently fired a dozen employees who failed their drug test, and I'm concerned that others might be hiding the drugs with all the magic teas they have nowadays.

Right.

 Now, I'm interested in a brand-new testing procedure I've read about that's a lot more accurate than the urine or hair tests. The new test is where a certain amount of flesh is removed from the employees to test for drugs.

I've not heard of that as of yet.

 You haven't heard about that. Do you think you could do some research and do that for a corporation? It's about four ounces of flesh.

Four ounces?

 Correct.

Are you sure, or is it four grams?

 I read about it in *Management Monthly*, I think they said it's about the size of a fat billfold.

You're going to take that much flesh from someone?

 They said it's a hundred times more accurate—it sounds like a great procedure.

Yeah, but do you understand how invasive that would be? Where are you going to get that much flesh from someone?

I believe they take it from the buttocks. Some of my secretaries could lose a few pounds and stay off the drugs, you know?

Well, I guess you can have some assurance that your drug testing is working if you've lost twelve prospective employees because they came up positive. Obviously, someone who is abusing drugs, if they're smart enough, can avoid the test. They can adulterate their sample in some way, sometimes where it's not detected. Most of the time, if a sample is adulterated, the laboratory can recognize it, and then send it back. They don't tell you whether it was positive or negative, because they can't, but they can tell you if it was adulterated, so obviously that's a red flag to you that this individual is using some kind of illicit drug, and that gives you the right to refuse their employment, because that's the same as refusing to take the test.

 Sneaky bastards.

But as of right now, the only testing that would hold up in court is the urine testing.

 What about the hair test?

There are some problems with hair testing, a couple of them. One is that it tends to be very race-specific, it's very difficult to test African-Americans with hair tests, so there's a bias built into it that way. Also, if you have someone who bleaches their hair, or uses very harsh chemicals on it, that's going to bleach out anything in the hair to begin with.

 That's why the flesh test is so interesting, because the fatty tissues save the drugs for many months at a time.

Right, and that's basically the theory of how testing for marijuana works, because it's stored in the fat, and as it's excreted out in the urine, you can detect marijuana use up to three months after it's been used, if the person was a heavy user.

 I've got the heavy users working for me right here. I can smell the drugs on them. I can just smell the pot.

Well, you must have a probable cause statement in your drug policy. If I were you, I would begin to take notes—days and times, and that kind of thing. Then, when you decide it's time, you tap that person on the shoulder and say, "Look, I want you to go down for a drug test, and these are the reasons why," and you've got some ground to stand on.

 Okay. Could you give me some tips on how to spot these druggies?

Do you currently do random drug testing?

 We certainly do.

So they know that at any time they could get picked?

 Right.

So that's a good deterrent. What you might want to do is step up your randomness—in other words, test more people more often—and that's perfectly within legal bounds as long as they understand that that's part of their employment.

 I'd like to institute random testing with the flesh test I read about. Besides the buttocks, I think there's an option to remove the pinkie finger for testing.

I've not heard of that, but I will definitely check around for you and see... Could I get your name again?

 I'm Mike Loew, and you can call our 800 number. (*provides number*) **It's a horrible problem here. I went into the bathroom just last week, and found two of my middle managers sucking on a bong. I fired them on the spot, I called the police—**

Uh-huh. Another thing you could do to let them know you're not going to tolerate this anymore is to say, "Okay, in the next month, I'm going to have everybody tested." You could call us, and we could come out to your site of employment and test everybody, and send it to the lab for analysis. And that way, within two weeks, you won't be smelling it anymore, because they're all worried about it. You test them, and then if you start smelling it again, you can come back in and test them all again.

 Could I get some dogs in here, to find drugs hidden in their desks?

If it's in your workplace, I think you have that right. I would check with your attorney about that kind of thing.

 Do you provide a drug-sniffing dog service?

No, we don't. You'd probably have to check with the local police for that. I don't know if you could use their dog, but they might know of someone who has a dog trained in that aspect. But those are some things that you could do. Let people know: "If I smell it, I'm gonna test you. And I'm going to tap you on the shoulder and you're going to come down to the clinic and we're going to test you."

 Sounds great. Well, if you could do some checking on that flesh test—

You bet. I will get right on that.

 Are there any other techniques on the horizon that we can look forward to?

I can't think of any. I think urine is still going to be the way to go. It's still very accurate. It's tough to beat. The teas that they drink won't do it. They might think it does, and they can drink all the water in the world, but it's not going to flush it all out of their system. Particularly if marijuana is the problem, and it sounds like that's your major problem—

 It's more than a problem. It's a terrible plague that's ravaging our nation.

Right.

 I mean, I'm sure you've seen it. Seen some horrible things in your time.

Yep, we've seen it.

 Well, I don't know if it could get much worse than this. I thank you for your time, sir.

DARE

 Hi, this is the neighborhood drug pusher from Los Angeles, and I wanted to complain about the negative light that you people have been putting us in. Kids have a lot of problems these days, and they don't need a hassle when it comes to getting drugs.

Female DARE Representative: Who is this?

This is Mike Loew. You know, when I come around the playground, all the kids are like, "Hey, Mike's here!" (*DARE hangs up*) Hello?

PIZZA RESTAURANT

 Hello, this is Dr. Mike Loew with the Pizza Industry Drug Usage Investigation in Los Angeles. I was wondering if I could administer a brief logic quiz to ascertain whether you are currently working under the influence of marijuana.

Male Pizza Worker: Are you serious?

 Oh, yes. Studies show that "getting stoned" is 790 times more frequent among pizza industry workers than the rest of the American work force. But I have a quick test, it's completely anonymous, it's even kind of fun. Would you like to take the quiz?

How long does it take?

 About two minutes.

Can I hang up at any point if I have to make some breadsticks or something?

 That would be fine.

Okay, sure.

 Great. And all of these questions refer to how you feel at this moment. So, right now, do you feel generally happy or generally sad?

Uhh… I'd say happy.

 How do you feel about the word "generally"?

Uhh… general.

 Right now, would you rather make a deep dish with extra sausage and cheese, or a thin crust with black olives and green peppers?

I would have to say thin crust because we don't have deep dish.

Are your eyes red or bloodshot?

No.

Do you feel like working right now?

No.

What would you rather be doing instead of working?

Uh, probably smoking a bowl.

While smoking your bowl, would you also like to watch cartoons on television?

No.

You don't enjoy cartoons?

I don't enjoy television.

In your home or apartment, are there patterned tapestries covering all the windows?

Hell, yeah. Not all the windows, but I've got some sweet tapestries, yeah.

Do you own a hand drum?

Yes, I do.

What type of hand drum?

A ceramic doumbek, which was thrown by a very good friend of mine.

Do you play this ceramic doumbek alone or in a group setting?

A little of both.

Do smells, tastes, sounds, and other sensory experiences have a hyperrealistic quality to you right now?

Uh, I'm not really sure.

Do you have a bag of tortilla chips in your home?

Nope.

 Do you plan on purchasing a bag of tortilla chips within the next week?

Probably not. I'm not a big junk-food person.

 Okay, that wraps up the quiz. Unfortunately, all indicators point to the fact that you are currently as high as a horse. Would you like to receive an educational pamphlet about the dangers of baking pizzas while under the influence of marijuana?

No, that's okay.

 Do you need me to "talk you down" from your "bad trip?"

I'm fine, dude.

 All right. Be careful, son. That sauce can get pretty hot.

OFFICE OF NATIONAL
DRUG CONTROL POLICY

 Hey, I'm calling for the Drug Czar.

Female Receptionist: Yes.

 Is he there?

Wait, I'm sorry, this is the White House Office of National Drug Control Policy.

 Yeah, yeah, the Drug King, is he there?

May I ask who's calling?

 This is Mike Loew.

And you're with—

You don't need to know that. I'm calling because I was there in Miami last night with the seventy-five kilos of smack, waiting for you people. The Drug Czar guy was supposed to be there with the ten million, and he didn't even show up.

I'm sorry, I don't understand what you're saying.

 I want the Drug Lord. I was on the wharf last night with the shipment of heroin that he was going to pick up, and he wasn't there. *(receptionist laughs)* What's so funny? The heat was on, but I still stuck it out for a couple of hours. Now I need the money for my other operations, okay? Put the Drug Czar on.

Are you a drug dealer, sir?

 You could say that.

Can you hold on for a second, please?

 Okay. *(on hold)*

Different Woman: Hello?

 Hey, where's the Drug Czar?

He's not in.

 Well, that's just great. Call him up and tell him to get his ass down here.

Where are you located?

 I'm here in Florida.

Where in Florida?

 In Miami.

Where in Miami?

 I'm at a pay phone right now.

And what street location is that?

Geez, I don't know. There's a McDonald's over there. But I'm calling because your boss lamed out on me last night—

Well, why don't you give me a phone number where I can reach you, and where you are located?

 It's not real cool to talk about that stuff over the phone. The feds are always listening, you know.

Is this a crank call?

 No, it's not a crank call—I've got a real problem here, lady. You ever drive around Miami with seventy-five kilos of smack in your hatchback?

Tell me where I can find you so I can have someone meet with you.

 Okay. How about—

And how they would be able to identify you.

 Sure. I'm a white male, about 6'4", and I'm wearing a big-ass hat.

Your name?

 Mike Loew.

Loew, L-O-W-E?

 L-O-E-W. Jesus, you people have to get organized. Get a Palm Pilot or something.

Mike, what is your phone number?

 (provides number)

That's not a Florida number, Mike.

 Well, I don't live in Florida. That's my home number.

And where is your home?

 Geez, why do you want to know so much about me? All I want to do is pull off this massive drug deal.

Because you said you were in Miami waiting for someone to meet you.

 Right. Very disappointing.

Mike, you specifically said you were in Miami waiting for somebody, and my computer now tells me you're not in Miami. Thank you very much, Mike. Good afternoon.

DARE

 Hi, I was cut off just now. Was I talking to you?

Female DARE Representative: Who is this?

 My name is Mike Loew, from Los Angeles.

Are you the neighborhood drug pusher?

 That's me. I just wanted to talk to you about your ads, where we're portrayed as demons and devils. Don't you think that's a little over the top?

Okay, this is your third time calling. Do not call here anymore with anything negative to say about our program.

 But I just wanted to have a dialogue about—*(DARE hangs up).* **Hello? Hello?**

To relax and unwind after these especially hard-hitting calls, Mike Loew is going to go get his crack on.

ABORTION ALTERNATIVES

 Hi. My wife and I live in a pretty remote area out here, and I was wondering if you could give us any alternatives to abortion.

Female Receptionist: Any alternatives to abortion?

 Yeah, we were hoping to terminate the pregnancy, but we don't really have the equipment or the training to perform the abortion professionally, so I was wondering if you had some other ways that we could get that done.

To terminate the pregnancy?

 Right.

Have you thought about adoption?

 Um, I guess we didn't think about that, really.

Adoption would be a very, very loving way.

 Yeah. We were just thinking that overpopulation is such a big problem in this world anyway, there just seems to be way too many humans. ·

Well, that would be for God to decide.

 Oh, I guess, but He doesn't have to live down here, does he?

He doesn't live down here?

 Right, it's humans that are living down here, and using up all the planet's resources and everything, and I just thought that another baby would contribute to that problem.

Well, would you be able to come here, and I could set up an appointment for you and your wife?

 I'd like to, but we live in such a remote area, and we have trouble getting transportation, actually. We don't own a car.

(shocked) You don't own a car?

 You're very good at repeating words. No, we don't own a car.

Where do you live, if I may ask, I'm not being nosy.

 We're out by Wausaukeewego.

Oh, okay. Well, just hold on one minute, okay?

 Okay.

(on hold for several minutes)

Different Woman: Hello?

 Hi.

Yes, um, did you have a question?

 Oh, this is someone else now?

Yes.

 Okay, hi. Yeah, I was calling because my wife and I live in a very remote area, and—

It's very difficult when people lie, you understand what I'm saying? And Jesus said, "Beware the Prince of the World, he was a Liar from the Beginning," okay? Abortion is about the murder of children, and we are about saving children's lives, okay? And you are speaking RUBBISH. You are speaking LIES. And I don't have the time or the desire to show that to you, okay? You're speaking RUBBISH, you are a married man, and you have conceived a BABY, and you are telling me that there's no room for the baby! Well, YOU get off!

 Isn't that what got me in trouble in the first place?

No, you get off the EARTH and then there's room for the baby! YOU get off the Earth, then there's room for the child! Do you understand?!? That's it in a nutshell, and don't bother me with your LIES! You are being deceived by SATAN and you are WORKING for him!

 Okay, okay, I'm working for Satan, you got me. Darn.

MY FIRST

MILITIA

Armageddon—the final, terrible struggle of good and evil that was foretold by this one guy almost two thousand years ago. Ever since that prophetic moment of divine inspiration, men have felt the need to hole up in a shack somewhere and start stockpiling weapons. Infiltrating the dangerous subculture of modern American militias, Mike Loew moved to Montana, built himself a nice compound, and began making preparatory phone calls for the end of the world.

UNIFORM STORE

 Hello, this is Mike Loew from Montana. I need uniforms for my militia—something rugged and outdoorsy. Do you have paramilitary clothing?

Female Employee: You're looking for military fatigues?

 Yes, with combat boots and tough pants.

What color?

 I need a prairie camouflage, with blended tones of beige, tan and brown.

Sure. They come in regular cotton twill, or you can get them in what they call battle rip-stop.

 Ooh, nice.

That has a nylon blend to it.

 Yeah, we do survivalist training outdoors for weeks at a time, and there are branches and sticks that can be sharp and pokey.

I've actually seen both of them, and as far as the rip-stop goes, it's just as good as the twill, and you pay more for the rip-stop. The cotton trousers are $31.95, and shirts also are $31.95.

 Can I get a group discount here?

That's as cheap as we can get them. Let me pull the file for you and see if I can get them for you in tan or brown.

 Thanks. Also, do you have snow battle suits?

We can get those from the same organization, yes. Okay, the trousers tie at the bottom and have an adjustable waist, just like the military ones. Six pockets total, two bellows pockets on the side. I also have a four-pocket coat, which is the kind you wear untucked, it's got two chest pockets and two lower pockets. I also have the short-sleeve and long-sleeve two-pocket shirts, that you do tuck in.

 Nice pocket selection there. How much canned food could I fit in those pockets?

If you're talking about the size of a soup can, I would say maybe one in the coat pockets, but two or three in the bellows pockets.

Can you customize these uniforms for me?

What did you need done?

I don't want any American flags on the shoulders. We have our own insignia.

Like an embroidery, or a patch?

How about a patch of our logo?

Sure, patches are not a problem. How many are you looking at?

I need thirty-three patches for all my followers.

Usually there's a minimum of fifty.

Okay. We're actively recruiting, so we should have more members soon.

What kind of design are you thinking about?

I can supply you with our logo. The initials are M.A.L., which stands for Montana Army of Liberation. Also, they stand for my name, Michael Andrew Loew, which is cool.

Okay, three letters...

And the letters are on an outline map of the state of Montana, which has wings on it, and the state is busting out of these encircling chains that also look like electron paths on a hydrogen atom, so the whole thing sort of looks like a nuclear explosion.

How many colors?

Red, yellow, and black. Three, please.

And all you would want on it is M.A.L. and that logo?

Plus a few verses of Scripture.

I'm going to estimate here—that would run about $4.95 per patch. You would have to buy all fifty of them right away, so that would be

$247.50. They keep your design on file for a couple of years, too, so if you ever need more, you could just let us know.

 We do occasionally lose faithful members. Can I get military dress uniforms from you, for the funerals and other fellowships that we have at the compound?

Actually, no. Anything that's more like an Army, Navy, Air Force or Marine uniform, I can't get for you. Have you seen the fire department's dress blazer? Double-breasted, two rows of buttons, it's a poly-wool blend, those I can get. Also, we have a wide variety of dress caps.

 That sounds too jaunty. How about those snow battle suits?

Oh right, you were looking for a one-piece also. Let's see, I have M65 field coats and the N3B parka. I have a shipboard coverall, but that's not very warm. The only other thing that I have is a flight suit, a Nomex flight suit. It's fireproof, eight pockets—

 Could we practice hang gliding in that?

You could. You're going to hang glide?

 Yes. Soon.

That sounds like fun.

 It's a good thing it's fireproof.

Right, it is made of Nomex, velcro adjustable cuffs, two-way zipper from the neck down, velcro waist-adjusting straps...

 Can I get those flight suits all in black, for stealth operations?

I think if you saw this flight suit, it would be just what you're looking for. The problem is it only comes in sage green.

 Is that dark enough to avoid detection?

No, not really. Let me pull up my color catalog. When I look at it, to me it almost looks like the color of—moss? You know, not a real light-colored moss on a tree, but a little bit darker? I don't know if that makes any sense to you at all, but I was just up north in the woods for a couple days myself, so... (chuckles)

Good for you. Unfortunately, we're not going to be hang gliding through moss.

It's kind of like an olive green, actually. That's about as close as I can come to explaining it. If you want to stop in some time, I can show you everything I have.

 Can I come in with all thirty-three of my men and get them sized for the flight suits?

No problem.

 Some of them don't get out of the compound much, but don't worry, I'll keep an eye on them.

Okay. Well, when you come in with your group, just ask for Brenda.

 We will come looking for you, Brenda.

HANG GLIDING INSTRUCTION

 Hi, this is Mike Loew from Montana. I want to learn how to hang glide, and I want to get my followers up and running on the hang gliders, too.

Male Hang Gliding Instructor: Okay, what's your organization?

 I'm with the Montana Army of Liberation. I'm the founder and charismatic leader here. I have a few specific questions for you.

Sure.

 Basically, we need to hang glide while holding a ten-pound device. I'm wondering how much weight a hang glider can carry in excess of the human pilot.

Well, plenty. Dare I even ask whether or not your Montana Liberation Army and this ten-pound device is something legal?

 Mmmm, I'll have to get back to you on that. Do you teach urban hang gliding?

Now that's not legal. You can't legally operate a hang glider over an urban center.

So I couldn't fly to the top of a building and then fly away.

No, not legally.

Whatever. So do you supply hang gliders? Can I purchase some from you?

Sure.

How about I just get some hang gliders then. I will pay you in cash.

Okay, but our policy is that we don't sell hang gliding equipment to people who haven't completed the certification training yet. So you'd be welcome to come out here and take our lessons, and get certified, and then we can sell you equipment.

Okay. What sort of range do your hang gliders have?

What sort of range?

Yes, how far is the striking distance?

Well, it varies tremendously. If, for example, we tow up 2,000 feet above the ground and then ride thermal updrafts, you might have 100 miles of range on a good day, and maybe only a mile or two of range on a bad day.

That sounds promising. So how much do your lessons cost?

Well, we have two different types of beginner lessons to get started with. We have hang gliding hill-flying class, which is what most people think of as a traditional start to hang gliding lessons. This is a $95 class, and it's a six-hour session. During this class, the first half of the class is ground school and skills acquisition, so we talk about hang gliding and then we do some warm-up practice running with the hang gliders and learning the coordination.

Does it look pretty scary when a guy is running with a big hang glider flapping on his back?

No, I don't think so. And the second half of the class is taking turns flying down a small hill until each person in the class has tried it a half-dozen times. For safety's sake, we don't fly very high the first day. Your longest flights of the day are going to be about the length

of a football field. You're never going to be more than ten feet up all
day.

**But eventually you work up to higher elevations? Because we need
to really get up there.**

Yes, we also have another type of beginner's lesson, high-altitude
tandem or dual hang gliding, this is where you go up in a two-person
hang glider with an instructor, and we go up to 2,500 feet above the
ground for private instruction.

Are these instructors good Americans?

Yes, they are. And the way that we get up there is very high-tech. We
use an ultralight tow-plane to tow the hang glider up gently but
firmly to high altitude. So you can visualize this, it's a rolling takeoff
and landing with wheels, so there's no running involved. You and
your instructor are in the two-pilot glider, and as the tow-plane
accelerates and lifts off, we follow the tow-plane through the sky like
we're water-skiing behind it. When we get up to 2,500 feet, we
release and fly free. And at this point, you take the controls and you
can feel out the speed and directional control of the glider. The cost
of this lesson is $125. And we have something called an intro
package, which is both of the lessons that I just described to you for
a package price of $199.

**So could I come out with thirty-three men and get lessons for
everybody?**

Yes. Would you like me to send you out a brochure in the mail?

Let's not leave a paper trail.

All right. When is it that you would like to bring out your large group
for lessons?

**I was hoping to do it within the next two months. We're really
gearing up for the year 2000 here.**

Okay, our season only lasts until the end of November, and then
we're closed until March 1.

So I would have to get in there pretty quick.

Yeah, you've got about five weeks.

I would need to coordinate that with the men and make sure we could all leave our posts at the compound. I am disappointed about the urban hang gliding, though.

What do you have in mind?

Basically, we're in the business of demolishing old government buildings. I was thinking we could fly onto a building that needed to be demolished, plant the device, then fly away. With some of these buildings, it's dangerous to get in on the ground, so we want to come in from up top, do what needs to be done, then cruise off.

Well, unfortunately, I don't think the aircraft exists that is going to give you that opportunity, with the possible exception of helicopters.

So even an awesome hang gliding guy couldn't do a pinpoint landing on top of a federal building?

Not without vertical takeoff and landing capabilities. I think you'd really be looking for a helicopter.

That reminds me—the black helicopters. Oh, God.

Are you all right, sir?

I have to call the Brazilians. I'll talk to you later.

Okay. I hope we'll be able to help you guys out.

EMBASSY OF BRAZIL

Hi, is this the military attaché?

Female Receptionist: Yes.

I don't think the hang gliders are going to work, so I was wondering if I could purchase some weapons from Brazil.

Weapons?

Yes, weapons. I'm out here in Montana, and lately the black helicopters have been circling in the sky, so I thought I should get some rocket launchers. I've heard that Brazil does their share of international weapons trading.

Okay, I'm going to give you another number where you can find out, okay? This is the Brazilian Army Commission. The number there is *(provides number)*. That is the main number. If nobody answers, just leave a message. Otherwise, let me see... You can try this number also—*(provides another number)*.

Okay. Now the first number is for the Brazilian Army Commission—

Both are for the Brazilian Army Commission.

Great. God bless you.

BRAZILIAN ARMY COMMISSION

Hi, I'm calling from my compound here in Montana, and I was hoping to buy some rocket launchers from Brazil.

Female Receptionist: You're hoping you could... Excuse me?

This is the procurement division, right?

Yes.

I would like to purchase some heavy weapons, please.

Purchase weapons from Brazil?

Yes, the woman at the embassy gave me your number. I was hoping to cut through all the red tape, and I've heard that you guys are ready to do business with your weapons.

Okay, first let me get your name.

My name is Mike Loew.

And what company are you with?

I'm with the Montana Army of Liberation.

Montana... Oh, now I understand, you want cheaper guns from Brazil, right?

I just want to get some rocket launchers, ma'am.

Oh, I'm just joking. Let me get your phone number.

 Sure. *(provides number)*

Hold one second.

(on hold)

Male Brazilian: Hello? My name is Colonel Ferreira, how are you?

 I'm feeling a little jittery, Colonel. I'm worried that the ATF might launch a raid on my compound, so I need to get me some rocket launchers. I want to cut through the red tape and get those weapons.

Okay, let me tell you that our business here is that we don't sell weapons. We mainly buy stuff for the Brazilian Army. However, we can arrange something for you, and put you in touch with the right people. I think we have a company in Brazil that produces this kind of material. By the way, they are here in Washington today. I have your phone number here…

 Is there a number that I could call, to get in touch with those people?

Yes, I don't have it right here, but hold on a minute. *(Colonel Ferreira holds a muffled conversation with someone in Portuguese and English, using the words "Montana Army of Liberation" and "rocket launcher")* Okay, the name is Colonel Carrança, and the company's name is Milibras. The phone number where you can talk to him is *(provides number)* and the other one is *(provides another number)*. Are you in Montana now?

 That's right.

Okay, there is a coincidence. They are here for this fair that we are having here in Washington today. Maybe you could talk to Carrança and arrange something.

 What sort of fair?

A weaponry fair.

 Do they have raffle tickets and free door prizes?

I do not know for sure… They have many things there, many weapons.

 Do they have weapons for sale? I have followers in the Washington area, so maybe they can—

Yes, they could go there, they can visit the Milibras tent and talk personally to Colonel Carrança. I think the fair is tomorrow, too.

 Fantastic. Where is the fair happening?

(Colonel Ferreira provides names of two hotels in Washington, D.C.)

 Thanks. So does Brazil make decent rocket launchers?

(lowers voice) I can tell you, they are very good. The best in the world. It is a very good rocket launcher. *(chuckles)*

 Wow. Better than the Stinger missiles that the U.S. makes?

Stinger I think is more of a missile, this is a rocket, not missile. It is a multiple rocket launcher, high range—I think it is a good one. You can talk to Colonel Carrança and he can tell you all about it.

 Do you think they could take down a black helicopter?

A black one, a green one, a red one, it does not matter. But Colonel Carrança can tell you more.

 I understand. So he's another colonel—is he in the Brazilian Army like you?

He is a retired colonel. Of course, the Brazilian Army has business with this company, but it's a private company, and this guy is a retired colonel, and he is with Milibras. He has been there a long time. He knows everything about the business, and he can advise you very well. And then, he can introduce you to different dealers in Brazil because he knows about our market there. We don't have all this information here, because as I told you before, our task here is buying stuff for the army, not selling stuff. It is a different business.

 So you stockpile weapons from various dealers here.

We buy everything, from weapons, to ammunition, to spare parts, to tanks, to guns, and medical equipment, computers, everything.

Could Colonel Carrança set me up with some tanks?

I think so. You can talk to him, he's a very nice guy.

 That sounds great. I'm going to call him right now.

And if you have further questions, you can ask me again, you can call me any time you want, and I'll be happy to help you.

 Wonderful. Thank you for helping my cause.

COLONEL CARRANÇA

 Hi, Colonel Carrança? My name is Mike Loew, and I've heard that you are the guy to talk to about buying rocket launchers.

Colonel Carrança: Who are you with right now?

 Just three of my wives.

So you need some rocket launchers.

 Yes, sir.

For what nation? For whom?

 For my group here in Montana. We're not an independant nation yet, but we're working on it.

Okay, let's see, perhaps I give you my fax number in Brazil. Okay, I'll be in Brazil next Friday, and you can fax for me about your request. That number I give to you... (*provides fax number*). Okay, you can fax to me, and I can give you answer, because by telephone is very difficult to discuss about the subject, okay? Where are you calling from now?

 From my compound in Montana.

Montana. Okay, is very difficult to come here to talk personally. Is much better that you can send a fax for us.

 Right. So what options do you have for purchasing weapons? Do you have a nice glossy catalog I could look through?

Yes, but I have here in Washington. You are in Montana—how can I do it? We work with several types of the 2.75, okay, air-to-ground or ground-to-ground, okay, and we have the launcher for this kind of ammunition, but I need to know what you really need, okay?

You need to know what I need to do with it?

That's it.

Basically, I'm sick and tired of the black helicopters snatching and mutilating all my cattle, so the next time they come around, I'm gonna get 'em. Can I use your rocket launcher to do that?

Perhaps so. I think so. Depends the requirement you have, okay, because there are some restrictions in Brazil government to export this kind of material, okay? So send a fax with all the information you can give, okay, and soon I give you answer. Believe me, next Monday, I give you answer.

So I should explain what I want to do with the rocket launchers— any other info?

No, no, only your phone number or something like that, okay? Okay, thank you, bye-bye.

A detailed and professional document, including Colonel Carrança's request for a telephone number (censored for publication to protect the compound) was earnestly prepared at M.A.L. headquarters and faxed to Brazil...

From the desk of General Michael A. Loew, Trail-Blazer-In-Chief Of
MONTANA ARMY of LIBERATION

December 31, 1999

My dear Colonel Carrango,

I think you are a very special colonel. Why, one might ask, if one (1) wanted to monitor my thoughts, are you such a special guy? BeeCOZ—MIK Lo Said So!!! Say that three times it's fun. You should sell me rocket launchers. Again WHY they always ask when at this verry moment the Rothschild/Rhodes Round Table/Rockefeller/Rosicrucian QuadRatic Equation solves the world's poplation problem with mass equatorial Xtinction using the Pentegon-engineerd AIDS bioweapon to create Lebensraum for the Freemasonic Supercapitalistocratic Elite in the face of the coming Ice Age. But you do not bow down to Their Frost. You are Carroobi, hero of Brazil! Together with M.A.L. we shall create the Most Monumental Moment Montana's Memory has ever tasted (5M Principle) you betcha the explosive birth of the 2000 Rockets. We'll have a big party! Bring your tinfoil helmet to S.H.I.E.L.D. against brain bombardment from psychotronic satelites manned by NASANAZI cyborg astronauts who used to be thalidomide children before They implanted bovine organs stolen from MY CATTLE! We MUST blow up many things before we all end up on te moon growing brain cells for THe Cobra Commmmmander. Below is technical diagram explainign what things must be explodded. MY pHOne NUMBER≠ IS: ██████████!!!! Give Me a call back, Buddy. I want rockets and misilesanpois; agfa;sag,gisaslk

—MIKE

MILIBRAS OFFICE IN BRAZIL

 Hi, is Colonel Carrança—

Female Receptionist: Just a minute, sir.

 Uh, thank you.

Different Woman: (speaking in Portuguese) Blah blah blah?

 Hello, I need Colonel Carrança.

Who is this speaking, please?

 This is Mike Loew.

Mi-kuh Lo?

 Yes.

From which company, please?

 I'm from the Montana Army of Liberation.

Maaaa—? Would you repeat, please?

 Okay. Montana—

Montana.

 Army—

Army.

 —of Liberation.

Li-ber-ation.

 Mm-hmm.

Uh-huh. Uh, Mi-kuh…

 Yes.

Uh-huh, umm, you have a sent a fax to him.

Yes, he received my fax?

Yes, yes, he has it... saved. But Mr. Carrança is not here today, he's traveling to another state, here in Brazil, and are you asking him to call you back when he arrive from this, this journey, okay?

 Okay, do you know if he liked my fax, or if he had any problems with it?

Uh, no. We don't have any problem.

 Oh, good. I was worried because I've been faxing it to you three times a day for a month now and I still haven't heard back.

Yes, but he have, he had, an adult, okay, and I will tell you, I will tell him, that you called back, okay?

 And he will then call me?

Uh, I don't think so, but if he didn't, please call us back, okay?

 Oh, you don't think he will call me?

Yes, because, he's travelling again, this week, and he had many, many meetings, okay, from here, and because of that, I don't think he for you have time...

 But time is running out. Is he busy selling rocket launchers to other people?

Yes, (laughs) he's very busy.

 He's moving a lot of rocket launchers for the holiday season?

Ha ha, I don't know, okay?

 Well, I sure would love to get some rocket launchers from your company. Is there anyone else that I could talk to about buying rocket launchers?

Ha ha ha, um, I prefer that you talk with Mr. Carrança, okay, then he will ask your questions, okay?

 Okay, does he have a mobile phone? A cell phone?

Mmm, no, ummmmmmmm, no. Okay?

 Well, please leave the message that I called, and my phone number is on that fax.

Uh-huh. *(nonverbal agreement delivered with a breathy, slightly ascending pitch, hinting that she is looking at the fax sheet right in front of her)*

 So, if he could give me a call back, with that number...

Uhhh, fax number?

 No, I left my telephone number on the fax sheet, so that should be on there, but I can also give it to you again.

Mm-hmm, okay?

 My name is Mike Loew, and the number in the U.S.A. is *(provides number)*. **Let's do this, okay?**

Okay, Mi-kuh.

 Don't make me build those rocket launchers by myself, now. Ha ha. Thank you for taking my message.

You are welcome.

 Have a nice day in beautiful Brazil.

For you, too.

 'Bye for now.

Mike Loew would like to ask the CIA to postpone his scheduled ice-pick lobotomy until after he has finished his book-signing tour. Thank you.